AAT

Level 3

Diploma in Accounting

Business Awareness

Course Book

from September 2023

BPP

Second edition 2023

Previous ISBN 9781 5097 4373 5

ISBN 9781 0355 0592 0

ISBN (for internal use only) 9781 0355 0493 0

eISBN 9781 0355 0638 5

British Library Cataloguing-in-Publication Data

A catalogue record for this book is available from the British Library

Published by

BPP Learning Media Ltd

BPP House, Aldine Place

142-144 Uxbridge Road

London W12 8AA

United Kingdom

learningmedia.bpp.com

Printed in the United Kingdom

Your learning materials, published by BPP Learning Media Ltd, are printed on paper obtained from traceable sustainable sources.

Contents

Introduction to the course

Syllabus overview

This unit provides students with an understanding of the business, its environment and the influence that this has on an organisation's structure, the role of its accounting function and its performance. Students will examine the purposes and types of businesses that exist, and the rights and responsibilities of key stakeholders. Students will learn what the micro- and macro-economic environments are and the impact and influence that changes in these environments can have on performance and decisions. This will include an understanding of the basic business law relating to the preparation of financial statements for different types of entities. Students will learn about the concepts of risk, types of risk and risk management for a business.

Students will understand the importance of professional ethics and ethical management, and how the finance function interacts with other key business functions to enhance operational efficiency. Students will learn the core aspects of the ethical code for accountants and will apply these principles to analyse and judge ethical situations which could arise in the workplace. They will also understand how acting ethically stems from core personal and organisational values, as well as understanding the legal and regulatory framework for anti-money laundering.

The role of the accountant is changing. This change is particularly driven by emerging technologies, so students will learn about types of technological changes that affect the accounting profession and the impact of these on performance, data analysis and accounting processes. An important skill for accountants is being able to analyse, understand and interpret information gathered and communicated in different formats. Students will understand the use of and impact of big data, the key features of blockchain, artificial intelligence (AI) and cloud accounting. Students will gain the skills required to visualise and interpret data to support understanding and decision making for businesses.

Test specification for this unit assessment

Assessment method	Marking type	Duration of assessment
Computer based assessment	Partially computer/partially human marked	2 hours 30 minutes

Learning outcomes		Weighting
(a)	Understand business types, structures and governance, and the legal framework in which they operate	25%
(a)	Understand the impact of the external and internal environment on businesses, their performance and decisions	20%
(a)	Understand how businesses and accountants comply with principles of professional ethics	20%
(a)	Understand the impact of new technologies in accounting and the risks associated with data security	15%
(a)	Communicate information to stakeholders	20%
Total		100%

Assessment structure

2 hours 30 minutes duration

Competency is 70%

*Note that this is only a guideline as to what might come up based on the AAT's sample. The format and content of each task may vary from what we have listed below.

Your assessment will consist of 7 tasks.

Task	Expected content	Max marks	Chapter ref	Study complete
1	**Organisations and ethics for accountants** Sub-tasks may test your knowledge of the following: • Types of organisations • Organisational structures • Control • Stakeholders • Corporate governance • Professional ethics	20	Types of businesses Organisational structure and governance Professional ethics for accountants	
2	**Analysing the external environment** Sub-tasks may test your knowledge of the following: • PESTLE model • Types of technology • Companies and partnerships The task is likely to include a written element, such as providing written explanations in an answer.	18	Types of businesses The external environment Technology and data	
3	**Technology, cyber risk and data security** Sub-tasks may test your knowledge of the following: • Cloud accounting • Cyber-attacks • Personal data • Data protection legislation • Service industries • Funding asset acquisitions	17	Technology and data	
4	**Ethical and legal compliance** Sub-tasks may test your knowledge of the following: • Ethical issues • Money laundering The task is likely to include a written element, such as providing written explanations in an answer.	10	Professional ethics for accountants Ethical conflicts	
5	**Microeconomic environment and sustainability** Sub-tasks may test your knowledge of the following: • Demand and supply • Sustainability	10	The external environment Organisational structure and governance	

 **BPP**

Task	Expected content	Max marks	Chapter ref	Study complete
	• Stakeholders			
6	**Communication and visualisation** This task may be an entirely written task requiring you to analyse data or information presented to you in a variety of forms. For example, you may be required to analyse charts or diagrams to explain the performance of a business.	13	Communicating data	
7	**Risk and big data** Sub-tasks may test your knowledge of the following: • Risk strategies • Types of risk • Data and big data • Decision making • Quality of information • Sources of information	12	Organisational structure and governance Technology and data	

Skills bank

Our experience of preparing students for this type of assessment suggests that to obtain competency, you will need to develop a number of key skills.

1 Learning and applying the theory

2 Logical approaches to tasks

3 Effective use of your time in the assessment

What do I need to know to do well in the assessment?

Like all Level 3 units, Business Awareness is a mandatory assessment.

To be successful in the assessment you need to:

- Understand business types, structures and governance, and the legal framework in which they operate.
- Understand the impact of the external and internal environment on businesses, their performance and decisions.
- Understand how businesses and accountants comply with principles of professional ethics.
- Understand the impact of new technologies in accounting and the risks associated with data security.
- Communicate information to stakeholders.

 BPP

Assumed knowledge

There is no assumed knowledge for this assessment, but knowledge gained from studying. The Business Environment at Level 2 will provide a solid foundation and background to what will be covered.

Assessment style

In the assessment you will complete tasks by:

(a) Entering narrative by selecting from drop down menus of narrative options known as **picklists**

(b) Using **drag and drop** menus to enter narrative

(c) Typing in numbers, known as **gapfill** entry

(d) Entering **ticks**

(e) Providing **written answers**

You must familiarise yourself with the style of the online questions and the AAT software before taking the assessment. As part of your revision, login to the **AAT website** and attempt their **online practice assessments**.

Answering written questions

In your assessment there will be written questions for you to answer. The main verbs used for these types of question requirements, are as follows, along with their meaning:

Identify/State – Analyse and select for presentation

Explain/Describe – Set out in detail the meaning of

Analysing written questions

Before answering the question set, you need to carefully review the information given in order to consider what needs to be discussed. A simple framework that could be used to answer a written question is as follows:

•   Point – make a point

•   Evidence – use the information from the question as evidence (if appropriate)

•   Explain – explain why the evidence links to the point

Don't forget to also provide a recommendation to management if that is required.

Introduction to the assessment

The question practice you do will prepare you for the format of tasks you will see in the *Business Awareness* assessment. It is also useful to familiarise yourself with the introductory information you **may** be given at the start of the assessment. For example:

Assessment information

Information

- The total time for this paper is 2 hours 30 minutes.

- This assessment has a total of 7 tasks which are divided into subtasks.

- The total mark for this paper is 100.

- The marks for each sub-task are shown alongside the task.

- Each task is independent. You will not need to refer to your answers to previous tasks.

- Where the date is relevant, it is given in the task data.

- Read any scenario carefully before attempting the questions, you can return to it at any time by clicking on the 'introduction' button at the bottom of the screen.

- Complete all 7 tasks.

- Answer the questions in the spaces provided. For answers requiring free text entry, the box will expand to fit your answer.

- You must use a full stop to indicate a decimal point. For example, write 100.57 NOT 100,57 OR 100 57.

- Both minus signs and brackets can be used to indicate negative numbers unless task instructions say otherwise.

- You may use a comma to indicate a number in the thousands, but you don't have to. For example, 10000 and 10,000 are both acceptable.

- Where the date is relevant, it is given in the task data.

(a) As you revise, use the BPP Passcards to consolidate your knowledge. They are a pocket-sized revision tool, perfect for packing in that last-minute revision.

(b) Attempt as many tasks as possible in the Question Bank. There are plenty of assessment-style tasks which are excellent preparation for the real assessment.

(c) Always check through your own answers as you will in the real assessment, before looking at the solutions in the back of the Question Bank.

Key to icons

Key term

A key definition which is important to be aware of for the assessment.

Formula to learn

A formula you will need to learn as it will not be provided in the assessment.

Formula provided

A formula which is provided within the assessment and generally available as a pop-up on screen.

Activity

An example which allows you to apply your knowledge to the technique covered in the Course Book. The solution is provided at the end of the chapter.

Illustration

A worked example which can be used to review and see how an assessment question could be answered.

Assessment focus point

A high priority point for the assessment.

Open book reference

Where use of an open book will be allowed for the assessment.

Real life examples

A practical real life scenario.

AAT qualifications

The material in this book may support the following AAT qualifications:

AAT Level 3 Diploma in Accounting and AAT Diploma in Accounting at SCQF Level 7.

Supplements

From time to time we may need to publish supplementary materials to one of our titles. This can be for a variety of reasons, from a small change in the AAT unit guidance to new legislation coming into effect between editions.

You should check our supplements page regularly for anything that may affect your learning materials. All supplements are available free of charge on our supplements page on our website at: www.bpp.com/learning-media/about/students.

Improving material and removing errors

BPP Learning Media do everything possible to ensure the material is accurate and up to date when sending to print. In the event that any errors are found after the print date, they are uploaded to the following website: www.bpp.com/learningmedia/Errata

These learning materials are based on the qualification specification released by the AAT in January 2023.

Types of businesses

Learning outcomes

| 1.1 | **The types of businesses** |
| | Learners need to understand: |

1.1.1 The standard organisation types and their key characteristics:
- Sole traders
- Partnerships (unlimited liability)
- Limited liability partnerships and limited partnerships
- Private limited companies
- Public limited companies
- Not-for-profit organisations including public sector

1.1.2 The impact of business type on an organisation's governance:
- Degree of separation of ownership
- Control/management

1.1.3 Types of funding used by businesses:
- New capital introduced
- Profits retained
- Lending
- Working capital

1.1.4 Common features of business organisations:
- A structure determined by groups of interrelated individuals
- Achievement of common objectives, ie goal congruence
- Cooperative relationships
- Defined responsibility, authority, relationship
- Individuals working together as teams
- Division of work

1.1.5 The differences between manufacturing and service businesses:
- Availability of internal information
- The processes and activities
- Reporting requirements

| 1.2 | **The legal framework for companies and partnerships** |
| | Learners need to understand: |

1.2.1	The key elements of companies' legislation:	
	•	The rights and roles of shareholders
	•	The role and duties of directors
	•	Regulates company formation and reporting
1.2.2	The key elements of unlimited liability partnerships:	
	•	What a partnership agreement typically contains
	•	That formal partnership agreements may not exist for all partnerships
	•	The definition of goodwill and its relevance to the partnership
	•	The impact of a change in partner on the partnership

Assessment context

In your assessment you will need to demonstrate that you understand the most appropriate form of entity for a particular organisation.

Qualification context

At Level 2 in *The Business Environment* you learned about 'Models of Business Ownership' and 'Business formation'.

At Level 4 in *Cash and Financial Management* you will learn about 'the importance of managing finance and liquidity, as well as 'ways of raising finance'.

Business context

Organisations come in a multitude of shapes and sizes. To accommodate this there are a number of different types of trading entity available to allow business owners to balance their needs for simplicity, privacy and financial risk management.

Chapter overview

Types of businesses

Why organisations exist

Unincorporated businesses
- Sole traders
- Partnerships

Incorporated businesses
- Private companies
- Public companies
  - LLPs
  - Shareholders
  - Directors
  - Financing

Introduction

When setting up a business the owner(s) will need to consider what form their business should take. This decision is important as it touches on a number of key areas, such as legal liability, the ability to raise finance, and the flexibility to expand in the future.

Assessment focus point

Exam questions will likely focus on three aspects:

(a) Can you identify the features of a particular business type, eg unlimited liability of sole traders.

(b) Can you correctly identify the nature of a business from the description given, eg the owners subscribed for share capital in a business in which shares could not be offered to the general public – this is a private limited company.

(c) Can you identify the most suitable type of business form in a given scenario, eg two owners who are not interested in any formalities – a partnership would be best here.

1 Why organisations exist

KEY TERM

Organisation: A social arrangement which pursues collective goals, controls its own performance and which has a boundary separating it from its environment. Boundaries can be physical or social.

Trading organisations are those set up to interact with other stakeholders, typically for the pursuit of profit. For instance, a manufacturing company will be formed:

- To source raw material inputs from suppliers
- To convert raw material into finished goods using machinery and staff to transform them
- To sell the finished goods to customers

The trading organisation will hope to do this at a profit, ie the value of sales will exceed the costs of the raw materials and the conversion processes.

To this end organisations, be they **sole traders**, **partnerships** or **companies**, are formed to promote:

- The pursuit of common objectives, eg making a profit
- To establish co-operative working relationships, eg between staff or in collaboration with suppliers or customers
- To organise staff into effective working groups, eg the finance staff will work together to produce the management accounts, and will work with other business functions to ensure good decision making
- To ensure adequate internal controls, eg each worker will be assigned by a line manager to conduct supervision and appraisals
- To ensure an effective division of work, eg staff are typically grouped by function, so that staff working in the same area work effectively together

The effective grouping of workers will be explored in more detail in the next chapter.

1.1 Types of business organisations

Business organisations can be created to serve several different functions:

- The pursuit of profit – this is the usual motivation of sole traders, partnerships and companies
- Charitable aims – raising money to spend on pursuit of noble aims, such as alleviating poverty or fighting disease
- Non-profit – eg public sector organisations seeking to provide services for the benefit of society (education, healthcare, policing etc)

Information is critical to good decision making. Depending on the aims of the business there will be different informational needs for its owners and managers, and this information can be sourced from a combination of internal and external sources.

Profit-seeking organisations will require information on:

- Sales, sales growth, market share
- Costs – sales less costs = profit
- Cashflow – how well are sales and profits translating into cash
- Customer needs – are they changing, are they being met?
- Competitors' actions – comparing products/services/strategies

Charitable organisations will require information on:

- Donations/grants – the main sources of finance
- Internal cost management – is the charity financially sustainable?
- Technical data – how well is the charity meeting their charitable aims

Non-profit and **public sector organisations** will require information on:

- Government policy – this will regulate their activities
- Economy – are they operating within their government approved budget?
- Efficiency – how efficient is the process of producing outputs relative to outputs?
- Effectiveness – is the organisation meeting its targets?

The final classification of organisations is the distinction between service and manufacturing organisations.

Service organisations provide intangible outputs ie something that cannot be touched or stored. Examples include:

- Healthcare
- Banking
- Accountancy
- Legal services

Services have the following qualities:

- Intangibility – the service does not provide a physical product
- Inseparability – the service is usually provided at the same time as it is consumed
- Variability – the service is tailored to the needs of each individual customer
- Perishability – the service cannot be stored and used later

Manufacturers make physical goods, such as cars, computers and foodstuffs. Here the emphasis tends to be on how to standardise outputs so as to ensure consistent levels of quality.

Activity 1: Hospital manager

Mena has been tasked with preparing a range of performance metrics for her hospital, so that its performance can be compared to other hospitals in the region. Mena has drafted three measures, but, is unsure how to classify these.

Required

Complete the table by indicating whether the following performance metrics relate to economy, effectiveness or efficiency.

	Economy	Effectiveness	Efficiency
The survival rate for breast cancer patients is 81%.			
Each consultant treats an average of 18 patients per week.			

	Economy	Effectiveness	Efficiency
The staff costs exceeded budget by 2.5% last year.			

2 Unincorporated businesses

Business: A business is defined as an organisation or enterprising entity engaged in commercial, industrial, or professional activities. Businesses can be for-profit entities or they can be non-profit organisations that operate to fulfil a charitable mission or further a social cause.

The simplest businesses are not formally created, they simply begin to exist when a person, or persons come together to trade. For instance, if you start to buy and sell cars to repair and sell on at a profit what you think of as a hobby may in fact be a business, and thus you could be liable to pay tax on any profits that you generate.

Businesses of this type can normally be classified as:

- **Sole traders** – a single person trading to make a profit
- **Traditional/simple partnerships** – two or more sole traders working together to make a profit

As these businesses are not formal, eg they are created without any forms being submitted to Companies House, they are referred to as 'unincorporated'.

Incorporation: The legal process used to form a corporate entity or company. A corporation is the resulting legal entity that separates the firm's assets and income from its owners and investors.

The main consequences of running an **unincorporated business** of these types are:

- There is no creation of a separate legal entity which carries out the trade, eg there is no 'company'.
- There is no degree of separation of ownership between the business and its owners, eg the business assets and debts are intertwined with the owners' personal assets.
- All contracts are made with the owners, meaning they can sue or be sued on those contracts.
- The owners will pay tax on their share of the business profits eg the salary drawn is not taxed in the same way as an employee. Instead each owner pays tax on their percentage share of business profits.
- The owners retain full personal liability for the debts of their business. This liability is **joint and several**, eg if one partner cannot meet their share of a debt the outstanding debt falls on the other partners.

Illustration 1: Personal liability

Billie and Jean form a partnership importing Jazz records from America to resell in the UK and Europe. They each invested £5,000 to get the business started, and in the early years the business profited.

Billie and Jean have just been told that their largest customer in Europe has entered insolvency and will not be paying their outstanding invoices totalling £35,000. The partnership has £5,000 of inventory, and £8,000 in its bank account. An invoice from an American supplier for £25,000 is now overdue, and they have sent a letter demanding payment within 21 days or they will seek repayment through the courts.

Analysis

As this is a simple partnership Billie and Jean are personally liable in the event that the partnership cannot pay its debts. At the moment it has cash and inventory worth £13,000 meaning that there is a shortfall of £12,000. In the event that this debt is not paid Billie and Jean could each be sued personally for £6,000 as equal partners. They could be forced to sell their personal belongings, eg houses/cars, to meet this debt, and if this is not sufficient to clear the partnership debts they could be declared bankrupt.

2.1 Partnership regulation

Partnerships are typically governed by a **private partnership agreement** drawn up between the partners themselves. Historically these have been very popular with professions like accountancy and law, as it allowed skilled workers to pool their expertise and resources to create firms with a wide range of services. Such agreements will regulate affairs between the members and should cover areas such as:

- Profit sharing, interest of capital, salaries
- How to resolve disputes between partners
- How to conduct meetings eg who is the chair
- Dealing with partners joining/leaving/retiring

The last point above is particularly important as in the absence of any agreement a partnership will dissolve if any partner leaves, dies or is declared mentally incapacitated. Dissolving and reforming a partnership every time a partner leaves could be very disruptive, hence an agreement that overrides this can be very important, especially in larger partnerships.

In the event that there is no formal agreement between the partners, or, the agreement fails to cover a particular aspect then the situation arising will be governed by the **Partnership Act 1890** (HMSO, 1890).

Some of the other rights accruing to partners per the PA 1890 are:

- To share equally in the capital and profits of the business
- To be indemnified by the firm for any liabilities
- To take part in the management of the business
- To have access to the firm's books
- To prevent admission of a new partner or a change in partnership nature

While at first glance these rules may seem reasonable, they assume that all partners are making an equal financial contribution to the partnership.

It is also worth noting that it is possible to create a partnership merely by starting to trade with another person. In these circumstances the people trading together may not even realise that they have created a partnership, and hence may not have thought to create a formal written agreement.

2.2 Goodwill

A particular aspect of importance in partnerships is the concept of **goodwill**.

> **Goodwill:** An intangible asset that is associated with the purchase of one business by another.

Goodwill is the portion of the purchase price that is higher than the sum of the net fair value of all of the assets purchased in the acquisition and the liabilities assumed in the process. It represents the value of a business's brand name, solid customer base, good customer relations, good employee relations, and proprietary technology.

Goodwill is especially relevant when partners leave and join:

- Partner joining – they will be expected to pay for the share of goodwill they are acquiring
- Partner leaving – they will expect to be compensated for the share in goodwill they are leaving behind

Illustration 2: Goodwill

Billie and Jean form a partnership importing Jazz records from America to resell in the UK and Europe. Each invested £5,000 to get the business started, and in the early years the business profited. As the business grows they decide they need more expertise and finance, so invite Michael to join the partnership.

The partnership's assets are valued at £100,000 and Michael pays Billie and Jean £50,000 each to buy his way into the partnership as an equal partner.

Analysis

Before Michael joins Billie and Jean each own a stake in the partnership assets worth £50,000.

Michael is paying £100,000 for a one-third share of the whole partnership, so must value the assets and goodwill at £300,000.

As the value of the partnership assets are £100,000 the excess valuation must be attributed to goodwill, which is worth £200,000.

Billie and Jean are each receiving £50,000 personally for agreeing to dilute their share of assets and goodwill from 50% to 33.3%.

The partnership assets of £100,000 and goodwill of £200,000 are now held equally by Billie, Jean and Michael in 33.3% shares.

Billie and Jean have made a taxable gain on their initial investment. They have turned £5,000 into £50,000 of cash plus a remaining stake of 33.3% in the partnership worth £100,000 to each of them.

3 Incorporated businesses

Given the risks of personal liability associated with sole traders and traditional partnerships many business owners prefer to trade using **incorporated entities**.

Incorporated entities are those that have been created by the filing of legal documents, and as such result in the creation of a separate legal entity, such as a company or limited liability partnership (LLP).

Once a separate legal entity has been incorporated it exists in law as a **separate legal person**, and hence becomes liable for its own debts.

This is as a result of the creation of the 'veil of incorporation', the legal concept that the company or LLP is a separate legal person to its owners. Therefore if the company or LLP is unable to pay its own debts then it is the company that is subject to liquidation, not its owners.

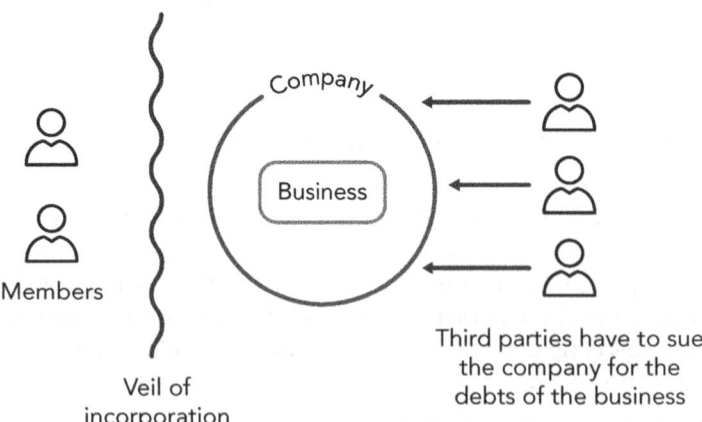

Illustration 3: Veil of incorporation

Billie and Jean form a limited liability company importing Jazz records from America to resell in the UK and Europe. Each invested £5,000 in the share capital of BJ Ltd and in the early years the company profited.

Billie and Jean have just been told that their largest customer in Europe has entered insolvency and will not be paying their outstanding invoices totalling £35,000. The company has £5,000 of inventory, and £8,000 in its bank account. An invoice from an American supplier for £25,000 is now overdue, and they have sent a letter demanding payment within 21 days or they will seek repayment through the courts.

Analysis

As this is a company it is BJ Ltd that is liable for the shortfall of £12,000. The supplier will be suing the company as it is the company that owes them money. In the event that BJ Ltd cannot pay the debts it will be liquidated. Any attempts by the American supplier to sue Billie or Jean will fail; they are protected by the veil of incorporation. In this instance they will of course see their company liquidated, and hence lose their £5,000 they initially invested.

3.1 Private limited companies

After sole traders, the second most common form of business arrangement in the UK is **the private company limited by shares**, often referred to 'Limited Companies'.

Limited companies are formed via the process of incorporation, and their legal existence is evidenced by the grant of the **Certificate of Incorporation**. This legal document serves much the same purpose as an individual's birth certificate, eg it confirms their existence, their date of birth and their name.

To form a limited company the following must be filed online with Companies House:

- Memorandum and articles of association – the documents that regulate the internal affairs of the company. The Articles operate in much the same way as a partnership agreement
- Application for registration – statutory form
- Statement of proposed officers – details of directors and company secretary
- Statement of compliance – an oath that all submissions are honest and truthful
- Statement of capital and initial shareholdings – details of the types, values and amounts of shares being issued to the initial shareholders

Once the certificate of incorporation is issued the company may lawfully trade from the date on the certificate eg it may enter into contracts in its own name and is liable for those contracts form that date.

Some of the distinguishing features of limited companies are:

- Its name must end in the word 'Limited'.
- Its shares cannot be advertised or offered to sale to the general public.
- There is no minimum number or value of shares that must be issued.
- There must be at least one director.
- If there is more than one director, then there is no need to appoint a company secretary.

An alternative corporate structure is the **private company limited by guarantee**. Instead of issuing shares the members of these rare companies agree to guarantee the debts of the company to a stated amount. In the event that the company faces insolvency the guarantee is the limit of the members' liability. There are no minimum or maximum amounts.

Companies limited by guarantee are allowed to exclude the word 'limited' from their name on most forms as long as they are a non-profit organisation such as a charity or research company.

3.2 Public limited companies

In order to obtain a stock market listing companies are required to become 'public' companies, often referred to as 'plcs'. It is important to note that just because a company is a plc, this does not mean it is listed. The plc status is merely a requirement of the listing.

A stock market listing allows the companies' shares to be traded; and opens up more financing opportunities for the company eg it can raise new debt and equity finance using the money markets.

In order to form a plc there are additional steps over and above the process outlined above for private limited companies. This includes applying for a **trading certificate** requiring:

- The name of the company must end in 'public limited company' or 'plc'
- The allotted share capital must be at least £50,000
- There must be at least two directors
- There must be a company secretary

Once the trading certificate is issued the company may lawfully trade in its own name, conferring limited liability to its members in the same way as privately limited companies.

3.2.1 Filing requirements

Companies limited by shares of all types must file certain documents with the Registrar at Companies House. These include:

- Financial statements
- Confirmation statement – confirming company officers and share structure
- Copies of resolutions

The responsibility for filing and legal compliance in general is delegated to the **Company Secretary**. It is compulsory for public companies to appoint a Company Secretary, but in private companies this is optional, unless there is only one director.

Although there is no statutory definition of the powers of the Company Secretary in the Companies Act 2006 case law tells us that the Company Secretary has the power to bind the company in contracts of an administrative nature.

3.3 Public vs private companies

The main differences between public and private companies are summarised in the table below.

Feature	Private Co	Public Co
Minimum number of directors	1	2
Minimum number of members	1	1
Minimum share capital	One share	£50,000
Advertise shares to public	No	Yes
Annual general meeting	Optional	Compulsory
Company secretary	Optional	Compulsory
File accounts after year end	9 months	6 months

3.4 Company directors

Although they are legal entities, companies clearly lack the capability to negotiate and sign contract themselves – as such the powers of the company reside in its board of directors. The board are empowered to run the company in accordance with its articles and in accordance with company law. As we will see below the directors are essentially able to run the company on a day-to-day basis free from shareholder interference.

The directors are however bound by a range of fiduciary and statutory duties.

Fiduciary duties are those imposed on persons operating in a position of trust. In essence a fiduciary is a strict duty not to take personal advantage, eg to act in the best interest of the fiduciary, not yourself. The fiduciary duties of directors are:

- A duty to account for any monies/goods/services received
- Avoid a conflict of interest, eg to always act in the best interests of the company, not themselves
- Duty to disclose, eg where a director receives an offer to do private work for a client of their firm
- Not to make a secret profit, eg not to accept money from a supplier to secure contracts

For instance if a director is offered a £10,000 payment by a supplier who is bidding to win a contract with the company this offer must be disclosed to the company and should be declined to avoid a breach of the fiduciary duties.

Statutory duties are those imposed by the **Companies Act 2006** (TSO, 2006). These include:

- To run the company in accordance with its articles of association
- To promote the success of the company, eg to sustainably manage the long-term profitability
- To exercise independent judgement, eg to be objective in decision making
- To exercise reasonable skill, care and diligence, eg to avoid acting negligently
- To avoid conflicts of interest – in line with the fiduciary duties
- Avoid benefits from third parties – to avoid bribes
- Declare interests in transactions – where a conflict interest has or will arise to disclose this in line with fiduciary duties

Where the directors are found to be in breach of their duties the following sanctions may apply:

- Termination of their service contract
- Damages may be payable to the company for any losses it has suffered
- Repayment to the company of any illicit profits earned
- Return of any property improperly taken

3.5 Shareholders

We have seen that the day-to-day decision making in companies is delegated to the board of directors. This creates '**separation of ownership**', ie the shareholders own the business but it is the directors that manage the company. Of course in small private limited companies it is common for the owners to also appoint themselves as the directors. In listed companies, however, the board are typically externally appointed and do not have a controlling stake in business.

3.6 Meetings and resolutions

The powers of shareholders are therefore exercised by voting on **resolutions** in meetings. There are three types of meetings that companies hold:

- **Board meetings** – These are conducted by the directors.
- **Annual General Meeting (AGM)** – The AGM is held once each calendar year by public companies. These are optional for private companies.
- **General Meeting (GM)** – GMs are held as and when required. These can be called by either the directors, or, by shareholders who control at least 5% of the company's voting rights. Where shareholders request a GM they will also have the right to propose resolutions to vote on.

At AGMs and GMs shareholder vote on two types of resolutions:

- **Ordinary resolutions** – These require a simple majority of votes cast at a meeting to be passed. These are used to approve the accounts and to appoint/remove the directors.
- **Special resolutions** – These require a 75% majority of votes cast, and are reserved for matters such as changing the company's articles or instigating insolvency procedures.

As private companies are typically managed by their owners they can dispense with many of these formalities by using written resolutions in lieu of calling meetings. A written resolution can

only be used by private companies, as these are circulated to the members. Once the requisite majority agree the resolution is passed. For instance to appoints a new director >50% of the shareholders would need to sign, to change the company's name 75% would need to sign.

Written resolutions cannot be used to remove a director from office.

 Illustration 4: Shareholder powers

Billie and Jean's company, BJ Ltd was so successful that they decided to semi-retire, so they appointed Pepsi and Shirley to the board in their place. Pepsi and Shirley each subscribed for 10% of the company's shares so that Billie and Jean were left with 40% each.

A few years later Billie and Jean were shocked to learn there would be no dividend. It transpired that Pepsi and Shirley had run the company badly and there were not enough profits to sustain a dividend. Billie and Jean have decided that they wish to return to the board and remove Pepsi and Shirley.

Analysis

As Billie and Jean control 80% of the share capital they can request a GM and propose a resolution to:

(a) remove Pepsi and Shirley and

(b) appoint themselves as directors.

This should be a formality as they have the voting power to request the GM and to pass the necessary ordinary resolution.

Note. As this resolution is to remove a director this business cannot be conducted via a written resolution even though the company is private.

3.7 Traditional partnerships vs. companies

Having looked at traditional/simple partnerships and companies we can now summarise some the main differences between them.

Feature	Partnership	Company
Owners personally liable for the debts of the business	Yes	No
Senior management	Partners	Directors
Requirement to register with Companies House	No	Yes
Method of taxing profits	Partners pay income tax on their share of the profits	Companies pay corporation tax on profits
Annual general meeting	Optional	Compulsory

3.8 Limited liability partnerships (LLPs)

As an alternative to companies or the traditional/simple partnerships, LLPs can be formed to allow business owners to operate through a separate legal person, known as the LLP, under **the Limited Liability Partnership Act 2000** (TSO, 200). These have become popular in the UK since their inception in the year 2000. This has allowed accountancy firms to move from simple partnerships, with shared unlimited liability; to a situation more like a company shareholder, eg limited liability for each partner.

The main features of an LLP can be split into those that are similar to companies, and those that are similar to partnerships.

Similarities with companies:

- Incorporated via Companies House
- Creation of a separate legal person – the LLP
- Designated members responsible are for filing documents eg the same function as a Company Secretary
- Limited liability for the members – limited to an agreed amount per partner (no maximum or minimum amount)
- The LLP's accounts are filed with Companies House and are potentially subject to external audit.

Similarities with partnerships:

- Partners pay tax on their share of partnership profits (the LLP itself does not pay corporation tax.
- All partners have a say in management.
- The partners may draw up a partnership agreement document to regulate their affairs; this is not filed at Companies House.

3.9 Limited partnerships

A very rare form of partnership is those created under the **Limited Partnership Act 1907** (HMSO, 1907). This Act allowed for the creation of a trading entity that permitted some of its partners to limit their liability in the event of a liquidation, subject to the following restrictions:

- The partnership must be registered with the Companies Registry, eg be incorporated like an LLP.
- One or more of the partners must retain full, **unlimited liability**.
- Partners with limited liability may not take part in the management of the business; and cannot usually bind the business in contract.
- Limited partners cannot, in the ordinary course of business, withdraw their capital.

The advent of LLPs has made these forms of partnership virtually obsolete. To benefit from limited liability an investor in this business forms is essentially a 'silent partner', eg they place their money into a business into which they have no saying. This is much the same as a shareholder in a plc. However, unlike companies and LLPs the limited partners cannot freely withdraw their investment, and the people that manage the business remain personally liable for the debts of the business.

3.10 Financing businesses

All businesses will need sufficient finance to trade. Cash will be needed to meet:

- Short-term expenditure, such as monthly salaries
- Long-term investments, such as plant and machinery
- Working capital. This is the cash tied up in the business operations, eg if you open a shop you will need to invest in inventory to sell. If you buy £10,000 of inventory for cash, and we assume it will take two months to sell this inventory at a 100% mark-up, it will take one month to generate the £10,000 in sales that you invested in the initial inventory.

Finance will come from two main sources, **debt** and **equity**.

Debt is any form of money borrowed and will include:

- Bank loans for fixed sums (sometimes referred to as term loans)
- Overdrafts, which are more flexible as you only pay interest on the overdrawn amount
- Debentures can be issued to lenders; this is a form of 'IOU', ie a promise to repay the debt at a later date, with interest payable over the period of lending

Debt is relatively easy to arrange with low borrowing costs if your company is deemed to be a good credit risk.

Equity refers to investing in a company's shares. When a company is set up the original investors exchange cash for shares, which gives them their stakes in the company. Where subsequent investment is needed more equity can be raised by:

- The owners buying more shares

- Selling shares to external investors, though this will dilute the stakes of the existing shareholders
- Retaining equity, eg reinvesting profits rather than distributing them as a dividend to shareholders

Activity 2: Types of business

Megan and Carli are both looking to set up in business.

Megan's business will be run from her garage, where she plans to make personalised house signs. The only significant investment will be her time as she already has most of the tools she needs to get started.

Carli will be offering tax advice to local businesses. Carli plans to recruit an experienced adviser to her team of four as she is aware that other tax advisors have been sued for considerable sums when they have inadvertently given their clients the wrong advice.

Required

Complete the following statements.

(a) Megan should trade via a [▼] .

(b) Carli should trade via a [▼] .

Picklist

- Partnership
- Private limited company
- Public limited company
- Sole trade

Chapter summary

- Organisations exist for many purposes, including profit making, charitable, and non-profit governmental to provide essential services.

- Simple businesses can be carried out via unincorporated entities like sole traders and partnerships. There is no separation of control and ownership, meaning that the owners retain unlimited liability for the debts of the business.

- Partnerships may be regulated by an agreement between the partners. In the absence of this the Partnership Act 1892 will apply. New and retiring will require the partnership to be valued to ascertain the value of goodwill.

- Personal liability can be avoided by forming an incorporated entity such as a limited company by shares (private or public) or an LLP or Limited Partnership. Incorporation creates a separate legal entity which carries out the business.

- Companies are regulated by their articles of association and company law. They are controlled and directed by the board of directors who operate under a range of fiduciary and statutory duties. Public companies also require a company secretary to be appointed.

- Shareholders exercise their powers by attending or convening meetings and voting on resolutions at those meetings. Limited companies can avoid most of these requirements by using written resolutions.

- Companies are financed by a mixture of debt and equity.

Activity answers

Activity 1: Hospital manager

	Economy	Effectiveness	Efficiency
The survival rate for breast cancer patients is 81%.		This measure relates to how effective treatments are.	
Each consultant treats an average of 18 patients per week.			This measure looks at how efficiently doctors are working.
The staff costs exceeded budget by 2.5% last year.	This measure looks at how economic the hospital is in respect of its budget.		

Activity 2: Types of business

(a) Megan should trade via a │ sole trade │ .

Her operations are small, and low risk.

(b) Carli should trade via a │ private limited company │ .

Her business is quite small, but there are significant risks, so she should reduce her personal liability by using a company.

 **BPP**

Test your learning

1 Describe THREE different aims that an organisation might have when it is created.

2 Describe THREE qualities of services.

3 Which of the following statements about the Partnership Act 1890 is NOT correct?

	✓
All partners will receive profits in line with their capital contribution.	
All partners will have access to the firm's books.	
All partners will take part in the management of the firm.	
All partners will be indemnified for any liabilities.	

4 Which TWO of the following are examples of fiduciary duties?

	✓
Duty to account for monies received.	
Duty to promote the long-term success of the company.	
Duty to exercise reasonable, skill, care and diligence.	
Duty to disclose.	

5 Which of the following statements is correct about companies in insolvency?

	✓
Shareholders are personally liable for the debts of the company.	
Directors are personally liable for the debts of the company.	
Shareholders and directors are both personally liable for the debts of the company.	
Neither shareholders nor directors are personally liable for the debts of the company.	

Organisational structure and governance

Learning outcomes

1.3	**Businesses stakeholders' interactions and needs**	
	Learners need to understand:	

	1.3.1	Different business stakeholders:

- Customers
- Suppliers
- Finance providers
- Owners
- Government
- Employees
- Regulatory/professional bodies
- The general public

	1.3.2	Stakeholders' objectives and requirements from the business
	1.3.3	Stakeholders' contributions to and impact on the business
	1.3.4	The relative significance of stakeholders to the business (including attitudes to risk)

1.4	**Organisational structure and governance**	
	Learners need to understand:	

	1.4.1	Organisational structure:

- Different organisational structures: functional, divisional, matrix
- The impact that the span of control has on the organisation structure, ie tall or flat

	1.4.2	The importance of governance in different organisation types:

- What is meant by the term 'governance' in a business context
- The impact of organisational structure and size on governance
- The difference between centralised and decentralised control

	1.4.3	The role of operational, managerial and corporate/strategic levels within an organisation
	1.4.4	The role of the finance function in contributing towards the operation of the other business functions and the organisation's plans and decision making:

- Operations/production

- Sales and marketing
- Human resources
- Information technology
- Distribution and logistics

1.4.5 The concept of risk and risk management:
- Difference between risk and uncertainty
- Types of risk:
  - Business risk
  - Financial risk
  - Strategic risk
  - Operational risk (cyber risk and reputational risk)
- Risk management:
  - Transfer
  - Accept
  - Reduce
  - Avoid

Assessment context

In your assessment you will be asked to assess the optimal way in which an organisation should arrange its workforce. Additionally you will be examined on who an organisation's stakeholder are, what are their interests and how can these relationships be managed. In respect of risk and uncertainty you could be asked to identify and classify risks, as well as identity or discuss suitable risk management approaches.

Qualification context

At Level 2 in *The Business Environment* you learned about 'Models of Business Ownership' and 'The different functions of an organisation'.

At Level 4 in *Audit and Assurance* you will learn about 'The role of internal audit in risk management' as well as 'The role of corporate governance'. You will revisit stakeholder and stakeholder management in *Internal Accounting Systems* and *Control and Credit and Debt Management*.

Business context

The efficient management of resources, including how to manage risk is a key challenge for managers. All organisations are looking to optimise efficient and the arrangement of the workforce is key to this. A major influence on structure is the need to manage business and non-business risks.

Stakeholders can have a major say in strategic decision making, therefore any organisation needs to understand who its stakeholders are, the level of interest they have, and the power that they can exert.

Chapter overview

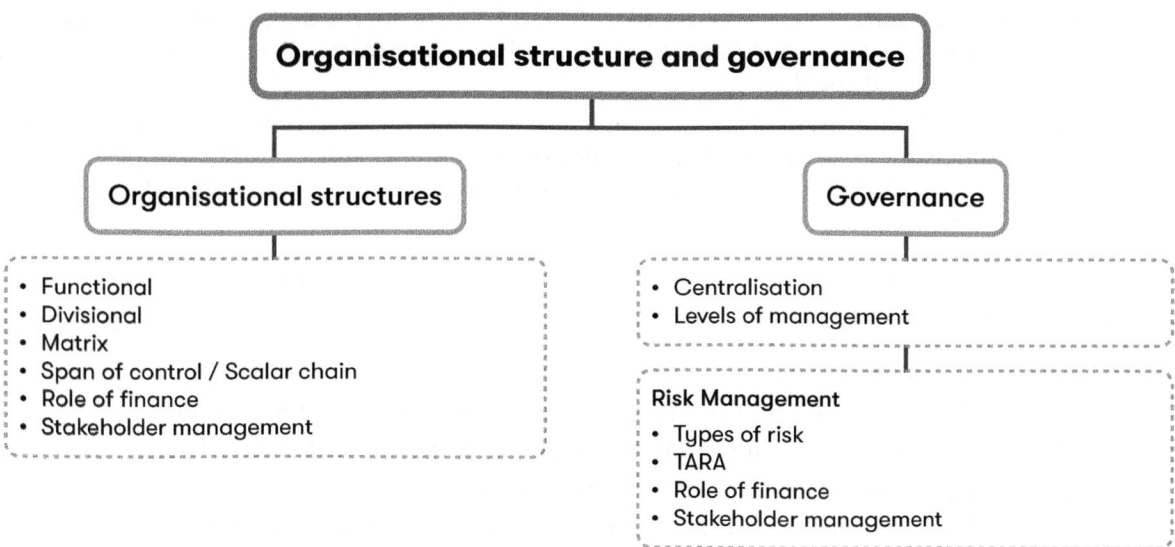

Organisational structure and governance

Organisational structures

- Functional
- Divisional
- Matrix
- Span of control / Scalar chain
- Role of finance
- Stakeholder management

Governance

- Centralisation
- Levels of management

Risk Management

- Types of risk
- TARA
- Role of finance
- Stakeholder management

Introduction

In order to run an efficient business the owners/managers will need to ensure that they organise their workforce appropriately. The resulting organisational structure will need to take account of a variety of factors including the geographic dispersion of operations, the organisation's culture, and the needs of stakeholders.

Another crucial factor will be risk management, how can a business balance the competing desires to innovate and change, whilst remaining adequately controlled? This chapter will explore the common risk control strategies, and how the finance function can contribute to planning and risk management.

Assessment focus point

Exam questions will likely focus on four aspects:

(a) Identifying the most suitable type of organisational structure for a company

(b) Identifying the most suitable controls required to manage specific risks

(c) Identifying stakeholders affected by a particular decision

(d) Identifying how the finance function can support other business functions

1 Organisational structures

1.1 Types of structure

Functional structures are created via separate departments or 'functions'. Employees are grouped by specialism, and departmental targets will be set. Formal communication systems will be set up to ensure information is shared.

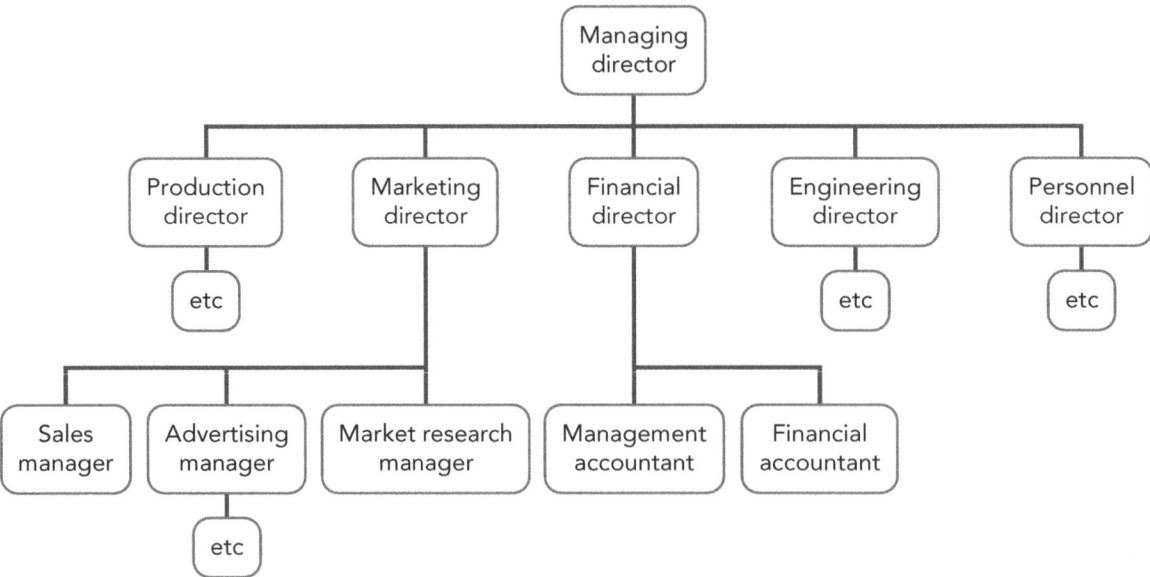

When organisations reach a certain size it may be appropriate to structure them into divisions or semi-autonomous blocks. These divisions may focus on a particular geographic area or a particular product.

An example of where the **Divisional structure** will be appropriate is where the organisation's activities are geographically dispersed, so that some authority is retained at head office but day-to-day operations are handled on a territorial basis.

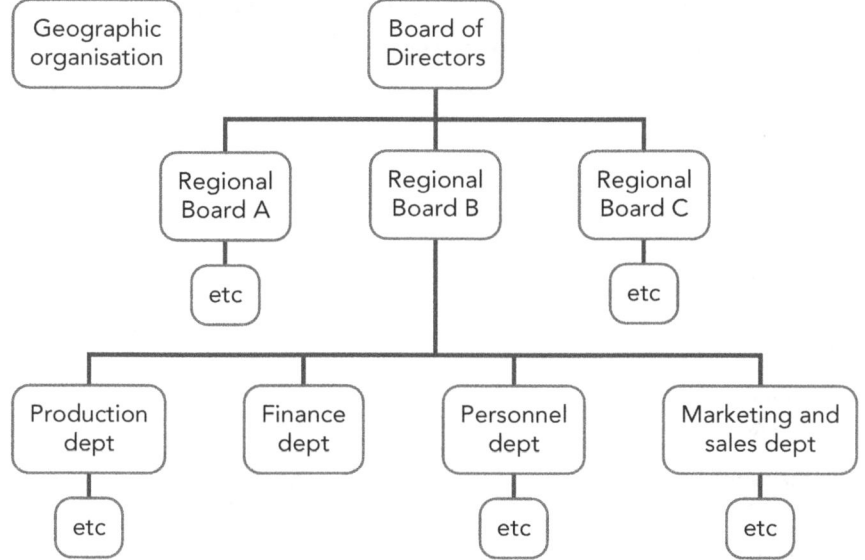

Divisional structures are also useful where a company makes different classes of products/services. For example a large accountancy firm may divisionalise are follows:

*   Accountancy
*   Audit and assurance
*   Taxation
*   Consultancy

Where an organisation requires a lot of cross-functional working, eg where the emphasis is on project management or innovation then the **matrix structure** may be appropriate.

A matrix organisation crosses a functional structure with a product/customer/project structure. This would be appropriate in an organisation where work is mainly project based.

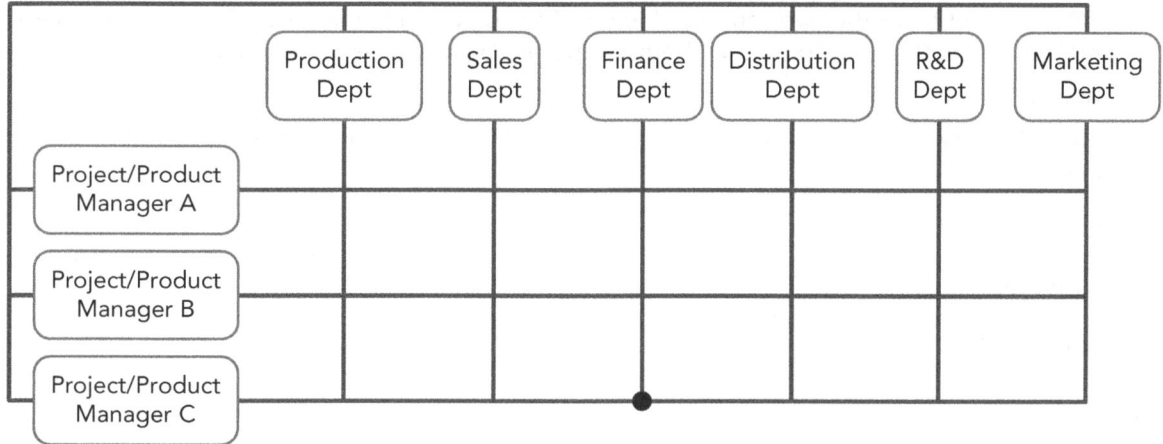

1.2 Span of control

A further influence on organisational structures is the span of control and scaler chain.

> **Span of control:** The number of subordinates that a manager can manage.
>
> **Scalar chain:** The number of links between the board and the most junior employees.

As organisations grow in size and scope, different organisational structures may be suitable. The scalar chain and span of control determine the basic shape. The scalar chain relates to levels in the organisation, and the span of control the number of employees managed.

Tall organisations have a:

*   Long scalar chain (lots of layers of management)

- A clearly defined hierarchy, each layer of management will have its own area of responsibility
- Narrow span of control; each manager has few subordinates

Flat organisations have a:

- Short scalar chain – fewer layers
- Wide span of control

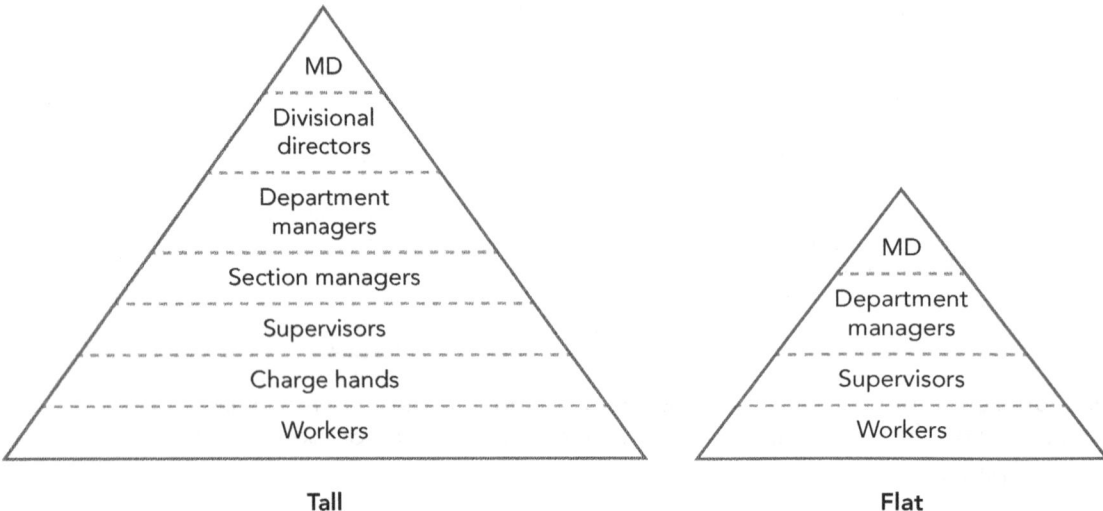

Tall   Flat

 ## Illustration 1: Scaler chain and span of control

Wasim and Waqar run a business located in Geeland and Beeland making hand-made sports equipment. In recent times there have been some quality issues and Wasim has blamed this on a recent move to widen the span of control.

When the company was formed it was agreed that each manager could manage six members of staff, in recent times that was changed to ten. The company employees 432 craftsman. Wasim and Waqar are the only board members, supported by managers and below them supervisors.

Analysis

Before the change, with a span of control of six and three links in the scalar chain the company structure was:

Directors	2
Managers	12
Supervisors	72
Craftsman	432

After the change:

Directors	2
Managers	5 (each can manage ten supervisors)
Supervisors	44 (each can manage ten workers)
Craftsman	432

We can see that the company could have lost as many as seven managers and 28 supervisors. This is a considerable cost saving; however, each manager/supervision now has more work to do.

The span of control can have a large impact on governance; as we narrow the span of control there is the possibility to delayer the organisation, which can lead to savings in terms of staff costs. However, this comes at the risk of loosening control.

There is no 'best' structure. All organisations must assess their own needs and adopt the structure that works best for them.

Activity 1: Corporate structures

Alpha is a consulting business. It employs staff across a wide range of functions but draws them together into cross-functional teams to work on client-specific projects.

Beta makes three very specific products, the Mars, Jupiter and Pluto. Each product has its own production facility and is sold to different customers in different markets.

Charlie manufacturers it's famous 'Wonky' chocolate bars. Its employs staff in a variety of roles such as purchasing, manufacturing, distribution, sales, HR and finance.

Required

For each of the companies described above indicate the most appropriate corporate structure.

	Functional	Divisional	Matrix
Alpha			
Beta			
Charlie			

2 Governance

Governance refers to the systems by which an organisation regulates and controls itself. This is especially important in organisations where there is separation of control. In these companies there is the potential for the directors to act in their own best interests, rather than as agents of the company and its shareholders. This is referred to as the 'agency' problem.

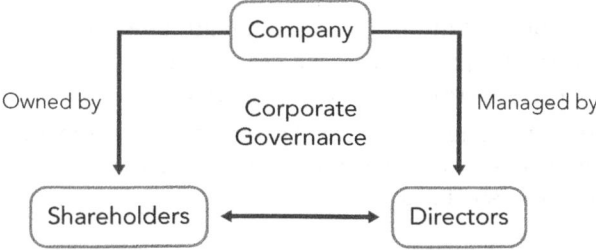

> **Corporate governance:** The system by which companies are directed and controlled. It considers how directors can be held accountable to shareholders for their actions.

Whilst listed companies are subject to formal control via the **UK Corporate Governance Code** (FRC, 2018), all companies will benefit from effective governance via:

- Risk reduction – this reduces fraud and the chance of the business getting into financial difficulties
- Improved performance – this should improve with the increased accountability
- Better company perception – this should improve as a result of strong control and thus may encourage investment

These improvements are driven by adherence to **key aspects of the Code** including:

- Splitting the role of the CEO and Chair

- Requiring a majority of the board to be independent Non-Executive Directors
- Not allowing the executive directors to set their own pay

2.1 Centralisation vs. decentralisation

A major influence on the style of governance, and the control that the board exerts over a company, is the degree of centralisation or decentralisation that is built into the organisational structure.

Centralised organisations retain much of the power and decision making at head office.

Decentralised organisations delegate more business decisions to divisional heads.

These approaches can be contrasted as follows:

	Centralised	**Decentralised**
Advantages	Faster decisions	Managers may be more motivated
	Holistic view of the company	Localised focus in decision making
	More control and standardisation	
Disadvantages	Loss of local view in decision making	Can be costly – need to employ more skilled decision makers
	Lack of autonomy	Can lead to strategic drift – loss of standardisation and goal congruence

2.2 Levels of management

Management and governance is concerned with the process of getting activities completed efficiently and effectively, with and by other people. However, as indicated by the scalar chain, the work within organisations happens at different levels. These levels of are typically subclassified as:

- **Strategic level** – This function is performed by the board. It is their job to set strategy and to monitor its performance with reference to how the business is performing, set against the context of the marketplace as a whole.
- **Managerial level** – This level takes the strategy and attempts to implement it into actions eg the design and sale of new products/services. They are responsible for managing operations and feeding back to the strategic level on the performance of the business.
- **Operational level** – This is where 'the work gets done'. At this level products are made, and services are delivered. It is the job of the managerial level to ensure the operations are running efficiently, and in line with the overall corporate strategy.

3 Risk management

> **Risk:** The condition in which there exists a quantifiable dispersion in the possible outcomes from any activity', ie the possibility that actual results will turn out differently from those expected.

Risk can be looked at in two ways:

- **Downside,** that something could go wrong and the effect is damaging; and
- **Upside,** where things work out better than expected.

When thinking about 'risk' businesses are generally thinking about 'what could go wrong?'

Perhaps more problematic than risk is the concept of uncertainty.

> **Uncertainty:** The inability to predict the outcome from an activity due to a lack of information about the input/output relationship or about the environment within which the activity takes place.

The key difference between risk and uncertainty is that risk is quantifiable, whereas uncertainty is not.

Illustration 2: Risk vs. uncertainty

Ross plc, a children's toy manufacturer undertakes some market research into a new doll, codenamed 'Rachel' and learns that there is a 50% chance that the product will be a success and will earn them £20m in profit this year. There is a 50% chance the product will fail, and the company will lose £5m.

Analysis

In this instance the company has quantified the good and bad outcomes, and can make a decision based upon their attitude to risk, eg can they afford to take the loss if the bad outcomes come to pass?

Without the research the company could probably guess that the product would be a success or a failure but would have no idea as to the likelihood of making or losing money. Faced with uncertainty rather than risk the decision would be much harder to take.

This scenario also illustrates the importance of good quality information in decision making. In this instance information has the ability to remove uncertainty.

3.1 Types of risk

There is no standard method for categorising risks. One possible method of categorisation is as follows. Note that some categories may be both strategic and operational risks:

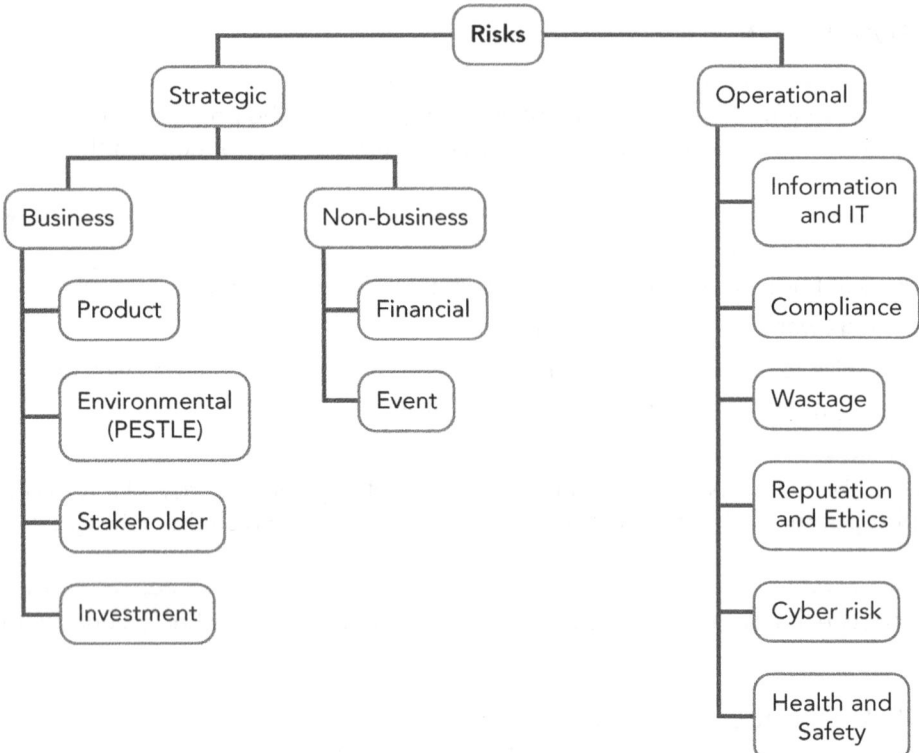

Strategic risks are those affecting or created by the organisation's strategy or strategic objectives. These tend to be long-term risks that the organisation is exposed to and are predominantly influenced by **external factors**. These could include competitor actions, or changes in government policy, eg switching from fossil fuels to renewable energy.

Operational risks are major risks that affect an organisation's ability to execute its strategic plan. These can also be thought of as the things that can disrupt the daily functioning of an organisation. These are largely related to **internal** factor, eg machine downtime, staff going on strike, industrial accidents, failing to comply with industry specific regulations, systems being hacked, or ransomware being installed.

Business risks are those that are specific to the organisation because of the industry that they operate in, eg product failure, poor investments, changes to the law.

Non-business risks affect all organisations, irrespective of the industry that they operate in, eg event risks such as fire and floods, or financial risks such as recession.

3.2 Risk management strategies

Depending on the severity and probability of the risks that they face organisations can adopt the following responses to risks:

		Impact	
		Low	High
Likelihood	Low	Accept	Transfer
	High	Reduce	Avoid

- Risk **transfer** – shift the risk to another entity, eg take out insurance.

- Risk **avoidance** – stop performing the process that exposes you to the risk, eg stop making a product.
- Risk **reduction**– implement controls, eg introduce quality control measures or additional supervision.
- Risk **acceptance** – accept that this risk of part and parcel of doing business, eg bear the cost.

You should remember this as the **TARA model**.

4 Role of the finance function

The **finance function** will often act as a shared service function, eg it exists to help other functions within the organisation. This is typically done by providing information and analysis that supports performance evaluation and decision making in those other functions.

Examples of how the **finance function supports others** include:

- Operations/Production – producing cost schedules. Analysing the contribution or profitability of different products or service lines.
- Sales and marketing – working out the cost benefit of sales promotions or marketing campaigns.
- Human Resources – helping to evaluate the efficiency, economy and effectiveness of HR strategies.
- Information technology – helping to evaluate investments in new technologies and systems, eg an analysis of cost vs. benefit or net present value of cash flows.
- Distribution and logistics – evaluating the efficiency of outbound logistics, analysing a decision to outsource this function.

5 Stakeholder management

> **Stakeholder:** A person or group of persons who have a stake in the organisation.

The definition above tells us that stakeholder are persons, companies or other organisations that will potentially take an interest in the decisions that our company is making.

Stakeholders can be very influential in terms of an organisations trying to deliver its strategy. For example:

- Banks may be required to lend money to enable a project to the undertaken.
- Trade unions may organise resistance to new working patterns.
- Customers may not like new products/services.
- The government may legislate in a manner that is unhelpful.

Activity 2: Stakeholders

Wasim and Waqar have decided to close down their factory in Geeland. They believe that production can be switched to their other manufacturing facility in Beeland, where labour, overheads and taxation are all much lower.

Required

Identify three groups of people affected by this decision, and for each briefly explain the nature of their interest.

Stakeholder	Nature of their interest

Stakeholders can be classified as:

- **Primary** – those directly affected by a decision, eg owners, managers and staff of a company.
- **Secondary** – those indirectly affected by a decision, who may still be able to exert some influence over the company.

Stakeholders can be further classified as:

Internal:

- Corporate management
- Employees

Connected:

- Shareholders
- Debt holders (eg bank)
- Intermediate (business) and final (consumer) customers
- Suppliers

External:

- Immediate community/ Society at large
- Competitors
- Special interest groups
- Government

5.1 Mendelow's matrix

In any given scenario stakeholders can be mapped on Mendelow's matrix in terms of:

- How interested they are in the company's strategy (might they want to resist it)
- How much power they have over the company's strategy (would they be able to resist it)

		Level of interest	
		Low	High
Power	**Low**	A eg Casual labour Action: **Minimal effort**	B eg Core employees Action: **Keep informed**
	High	C eg Institutional shareholder Action: **Keep satisfied**	D eg Main suppliers Action: **Key players**

The matrix is therefore a very useful tool in helping to:

- Identify stakeholders who are likely to be affected by a particular decision.
- Assess each stakeholder's likely reaction to the decision eg support/neutral/object.
- Evaluate the policies or actions that may ease the acceptance of the strategy.

Illustration 3: Stakeholder analysis

The Government is considering an outright ban on the sale of new gas boilers as part of its drive to make the country carbon neutral. As a result any new or replacement boiler installations would need to use heat-pump technology, which is more expensive than existing gas-fired technology.

Required

Who may be affected by this decision?

Solution

Analysis

- People with heat-pump boilers – minimal effort. They already have the new technology so are unaffected by this decision.

- Boiler manufacturers – keep informed. They are unlikely to be able to block the decision so must keep abreast of the new law so that they can get ready to comply with it.

- People with old boilers – keep satisfied. Governments must win elections to change the law, so any move that alienates voters, who may be faced with expensive upgrades, may be unpopular with the electorate.

- MPs – key players. Although the Government will draft and propose the new legislation it is Parliament that will vote on accepting/rejecting/modifying the new law. Without the support of a majority of MPs the proposed law change will be defeated.

Chapter summary

- Organisational structure is key to ensuring a productive and efficient workforce.
- Common structures include functional, divisional and matrix structures. Each organisation will need to find a structure that works well for them.
- A major influence on structure is the span of control, which impacts upon the scalar chain.
- Governance refers to how organisations are managed and controlled. This is especially important where there is separation of control and ownership, which gives rise to the agency problem.
- A key governance decision will be the balance between centralising and decentralising decision making.
- Management takes place at three levels of the organisation – strategic (corporate), managerial and operational.
- Risks can be good (upside) or bad (downside) and can be quantified. Uncertainty cannot be quantified.
- Common risk management strategies include Transfer, Avoid, Reduce and Accept.
- Risks can be categorised as strategic vs. operational, and business vs. non-business.
- The finance function will assist other business functions, such as operations, sales, HR, IT and distribution by providing information for performance management and decision making.
- Stakeholders are those that are directly (primary) or indirectly (secondary) affected by a decision made by an organisation. They can be categorised as internal (staff), connected (source of finance) or external (others).
- Stakeholder relations can be managed by assessing the power and interest of each group. Stakeholders can be classified according to action needed as minimal effort, keep informed, keep satisfied or key players.

Activity answers

Activity 1: Corporate structures

	Functional	Divisional	Matrix
Alpha			The cross-functional team working is suited to the matrix structure.
Beta		Each of the three products should be managed within its own division.	
Charlie	The scenario describes a range of functions that support a single product.		

Activity 2: Stakeholders

Examples of stakeholders could include, but would not be limited to:

Stakeholder	Nature of their interest
Employees in Geeland	They are losing their jobs.
Employees in Beeland	There might be more job opportunities.
Local community in Geeland	Local unemployment may rise reducing demand for shops, leisure and other services.
Government in Geeland	There may be more unemployment increasing state benefits, there will also be a loss of tax revenue.
Supplier in Geeland	They may lose custom supplying the factory in Geeland when it shuts.

Test your learning

1 Company Theta is a large consultant firm. They provide bespoke services to a wide range of clients incorporating accounting, tax, human resources, internal audit, IT and legal services. Each client is serviced by specially created multidisciplinary teams of experts.

Required

Which of the following would be the most suitable structure for Company Theta?

	✓
Divisional	
Functional	
Matrix	

2 **Complete this sentence:**

A _____ span of control will result in long scalar chain.

3 **Which of the following is an advantage of a decentralised organisations?**

	✓
Faster decisions	
Holistic view of the organisation	
More standardisation	
Increased motivation of junior managers	

4 **Cyber-risks are an example of?**

	✓
Strategic risks	
Operational risks	
Business risks	
Non-business risks	

5 **Describe the difference between primary and secondary stakeholders.**

3   The external environment

Learning outcomes

2.1	**The use of PESTLE model for analysing the external environment**

Learners need to understand:

2.1.1	The use of PESTLE to analyse the impact of the business's macro environment

2.1.2	Political factors affecting a business:
	• Government policy
	• Taxation
	• Imports and exports
	• Public spending

2.1.3	Economic factors affecting a business:
	• Interest rates
	• Exchange rates
	• Changes in disposable income
	• Business cycles
	• Demand-pull and cost-push inflation

2.1.4	Social factors affecting a business:
	• Demographic changes
	• Trends
	• Unemployment

2.1.5	Technological factors affecting a business:
	• Changes in technology
	• Impact on structure

2.1.6	Legal factors affecting a business:
	• Trade regulations
	• Changes in law and regulations

2.1.7	Environmental factors affecting a business:
	• Environmental changes
	• Sustainability

Learners need to be able to:

2.1.8	Identify PESTLE factors affecting a business

| | 2.1.9 | Recognise the impact of PESTLE factors on the business |

2.2	**The micro-economic environment**	
	Learners need to understand:	

| | 2.2.1 | The concept of supply and demand |

| | 2.2.2 | How prices are determined by the price mechanism (supply = demand, i.e. shifts along the supply/demand curves) and market forces (shifts of the supply/demand curves) and the impact of the type of goods (normal, necessity, substitute and complementary) |

| | 2.2.3 | The impact of price changes on volumes, revenues, costs and profitability |

| | 2.2.4 | How the levels of competition in the micro-economic environment are influenced: |

- Product features
- Number of sellers and buyers
- Barriers to entry, ie licences and regulatory controls, cost to set up, expertise
- Location
- Availability of information

2.3	**The importance of sustainability**	
	Learners need to understand:	

| | 2.3.1 | The meaning of sustainability |

| | 2.3.2 | The three aspects of sustainable performance: |

- Social
- Ecological/environmental
- Economic/financial

| | 2.3.3 | The importance of: |

- Taking a long-term view and allowing the needs of present generations to be met without compromising the ability of future generations to meet their own needs
- Considering the needs of the organisation's wider stakeholders
- Long-term responsible management and use of resources
- Operating sustainably in relation to products and services, customers, employees, the workplace, the supply chain and business functions and processes
- The accountant's public interest duty to protect society as a whole and the organisation's sustainability

Assessment context

In your assessment you will be asked to demonstrate that you understand the basics of macro- and micro-economics, eg what is going on outside of your organisation, and the laws of supply, demand and pricing. Alongside you will need to demonstrate that you understand the concept of sustainability, and what this means for the accountant in business.

Qualification context

At Level 2 in *The Business Environment* you learned about 'The economic environment' and 'Sustainability and the environment'.

At Level 4 in *Internal Accounting Systems and Controls* you will learn about 'the importance of ethics and sustainability within the accounting function' and how technology can support the reporting of sustainability.

Business context

Business owners need to understand what is going on around their organisations in order to make good decisions. For instance there is no use trying to raise prices if the providers of identical goods are cutting theirs. Likewise managers need to understand what sustainability means for their business, especially the costs and benefits of any proposed sustainability strategies.

Chapter overview

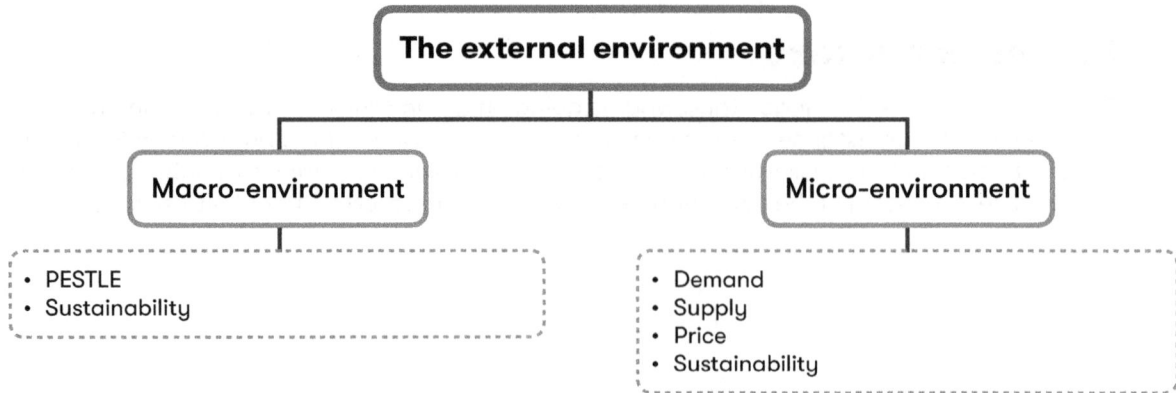

The external environment

Macro-environment
- PESTLE
- Sustainability

Micro-environment
- Demand
- Supply
- Price
- Sustainability

BPP

Introduction

All organisations exist within the wider environment, which will represent a source of opportunities and threats. As such it is important to scan the environment so that opportunities can be exploited, and threats mitigated. The environment is also subject to change, so will need to be constantly monitored to ensure the organisation's strategies remain valid.

An important new concept is the idea that an organisation's activities should be 'sustainable', ie it should be able to continue indefinitely without exhausting the earth's natural resources.

> ## Assessment focus point
>
> Exam questions will likely focus on these aspects:
> (a) Identifying environmental threats and opportunities
> (b) Explaining the actions an organisation can take to mitigate threats and exploit opportunities
> (c) Explaining how the laws of supply and demand will result in the equilibrium price of goods
> (d) Explaining the impact of various factors on the supply and demand curves
> (e) Explaining the importance of sustainability in business
> (f) Identifying the steps organisations can take to improve their sustainability

1 PESTLE analysis

PESTLE analysis looks at an organisation's macro-environment. This is crucial as the environment is subject to change, and these changes may invalidate the organisation's existing strategic plans.

> **KEY TERM**
>
> **Macro-environment:** The condition that exists in the economy as a whole, rather than in a particular sector or region. In general, the macro economic environment includes trends in the gross domestic product (GDP), inflation, employment, spending, and monetary and fiscal policy.

When conducting a **PESTLE analysis** there are three stages to consider.
(a) Identify relevant factors under each heading.
(b) Consider how these factors impact upon the organisation.
(c) Formulate appropriate ways for the organisation to respond to those factors.

1.1 Political factors

Political policies that can affect organisations include, but are not limited to:

- **Government policy** changes – Governments may make changes that impact upon an organisation's business model, eg if a government legislates to ban the sale of new petrol and diesel cars this will force automotive companies to switch to the production of electric vehicles.
- **Taxation** – Any increase in business taxes will reduce the funds available for organisations to reinvest in operations or pay to shareholders as a dividend. This could include corporation taxes as well as indirect taxes such as VAT.
- **Imports and exports** – Governments can impose tariffs and quotas to protect domestic production, eg to protect local farmers a government may impose tariffs of 40% on imported beef. Such moves are designed to make imports more expensive and less attractive than domestic products.
- **Public spending** – The government has enormous spending power. Should a government wish to stimulate its economy it can borrow money to fuel spending on new roads, hospitals and schools etc. This provides employment opportunities as well as stimulating supply chains.

1.2 Economic factors

Common economic factors that can affect organisations include, but are not limited to:

- **Interest rates** – The impact of rate changes can be quite complex. If interest rates rise, and a company has borrowed money with variable rates loans, these will become more expensive, reducing the company's cashflows. At the same time consumers may be faced with more expensive mortgages and have less money to spend, reducing demand for goods and services. The reverse is true for companies with surplus funds, and consumers with savings.

- **Inflation** – This refers to the rate at which prices are rising. As a rule high levels of inflation are undesirable as wages will rarely rise as quickly as the price of goods and services, so consumers will be worse off. Inflation can be driven by (i) demand-pull eg demand for goods/services is outstripping supply, or (ii) cost-push – the costs of producing goods/services rises. The typical response to higher inflation is a rise in interest rates, to reduce consumer incomes and dampen demand.

- **Exchange rates** – If the value of a domestic currency falls this will make imported goods more expensive to purchase, but exports will be cheaper for overseas buyers. Importers tend to favour strong domestic exchange rates, and exporters prefer weaker rates.

- **Changes in disposable income** – The net effect of interest rates, inflation, and taxation polices will impact the available money consumers have to spend on necessities and luxuries. As incomes fall the producers of luxury goods will see demand fall.

- **Business cycles** – There are established cycles that follow the rise and fall of the general economy, eg growth–boom–recession–depression–growth...

1.3 Social factors

Common social factors that can affect organisations include, but are not limited to:

- **Demographic changes** – This refers to societal changes that influence buyer behaviour. Relevant factors can include changes to the age, gender balance and ethnicity of a population. For example, over time the UK the population has become older due to improvements in healthcare standards. This means there are many more people of pensionable age.

- **Trends** – An obvious trend over the last number of decades is the rise of the internet as a shopping and marketing channel. This has created increased competition for traditional high street retailers.

- **Unemployment** – This is a particular challenge for governments. High unemployment is a drag on economic productivity. Firstly there are large numbers of people with very low disposable incomes, depressing consumer spending. Secondly the government is generating lower levels of payroll taxation, at the same time that it has a higher social security bill.

1.4 Technological factors

Common technological factors that can affect organisations include, but are not limited to:

- **Internet 2.0** – The second generation of the internet is now interactive. Users are creating and editing content, not just reading and downloading content.

- **Fourth industrial revolution** – We are in a new industrial revolution powered by digital technology.

- **Impact on structure** – The ability to work remotely using the internet, cloud computing and virtual private networks has changed organisational structures eg workforces are increasingly homebased and mobile. At the extremes virtual organisations exist. These consist of geographically dispersed individuals, teams, companies or stakeholders. The organisation usually only exists electronically on the internet, without any physical premises.

1.5 Legal factors

Common legal factors that can affect organisations include, but are not limited to:

- **Trade regulations** – Laws that are directed at specific industries can be highly disruptive. For instance, Brexit has seen many changes for companies that import and export from the UK

into the EU. As an example some goods now have tariffs applied when they are imported into the UK. This presents a problem for importers, and an opportunity for domestic producers.

- **Changes in laws and regulations** – General changes in the legal framework can also be disruptive, even when not targeted at specific industries. For example the UK government's commitment to making the country carbon neutral will have a massive influence on consumer behaviour, which in turn will require companies to change their processes.

1.6 Environmental factors

Common environmental factors that can affect organisations include, but are not limited to:

- **Environmental changes** – Changes to the physical environment can challenge existing strategies. For instance, the increase in more extreme weather phenomena exposes organisations to more event risks.
- **Sustainability** – Consumers are becoming increasingly aware of the impact that their environmental consumption is having on future generations. This can be a threat to companies unable or unwilling to change, conversely it is an opportunity for others able to satisfy demand for sustainable products and services.

Activity 1: PESTLE analysis

B City University offers a full range of courses to both full-time and part-time students.

In recent years employers have complained that graduates lack the skills necessary to make a seamless transition into work. They claim that they are having to run additional training courses to help bridge these skills gaps. Some large employers are increasing the number of school-leavers they employ.

The Government is mindful of the cost of supporting higher education, and the burden on taxpayers who do not attend university. To address this unfairness they are proposing a large increase in the cost of university courses and offering long-term loans to help graduates pay for their education over the first 20 years of employment.

B City University has noticed an increase in demand for online courses from part-time students. However, the University does not have the infrastructure to offer all of its courses online.

Required

(1) For each of the three specified PESTLE categories (Social, Economic, Technological) identify ONE threat facing B City University.

(2) Explain ONE action B City University could take to reduce threats under each category.

	Threat – identify briefly	Action to reduce the threat – explain what the University can do
Social		
Economic		
Technological		

Please note, you would not need the detailed explanations we have provided here.

2 Micro-economic environment – demand

2.1 Nature of a market

A **market** consists of all of the buyers and sellers of a good or service, or a factor of production (a resource required for production to take place, eg labour, land).

The price and output decisions of a firm will be affected by **market forces**, ie the behaviour of consumers and suppliers.

2.2 Demand

Demand is the amount (quantity) which consumers are willing and able to purchase of a certain good at a given price over a certain time period.

KEY
TERM

> **The law of demand:** As the price of a good falls, all other things being equal, the quantity demanded of that good increases.

The **law of demand** can be illustrated as a **demand curve**.

Illustration 1: Demand curve

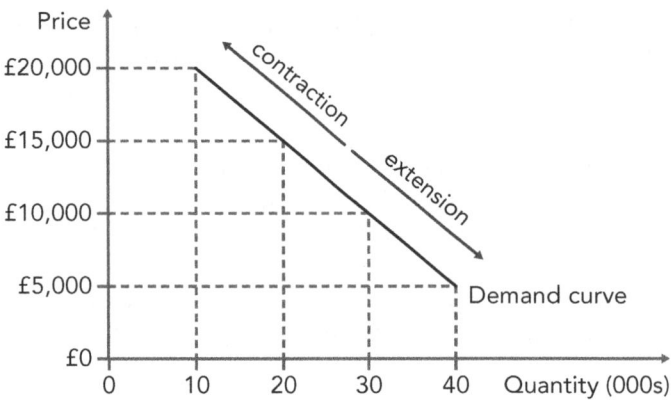

As an example, the diagram shows the demand for Mini cars.

- If the price is £20,000/unit: demand is 10,000 pa
- If the price is £15,000/unit: demand is 20,000 pa
- If the price is £10,000/unit: demand is 30,000 pa
- If the price is £5,000/unit: demand is 40,000 pa

The demand curve slopes downwards from left to right, reflecting an inverse relationship between price and quantity.

(a) **Extension (or expansion) of demand**: Increase in quantity demanded because price has fallen. Shown by a rightward movement **along** the existing curve.

(b) **Contraction of demand**: Decrease in quantity demanded because price has risen. Shown by a leftward movement **along** the curve.

2.3 Explaining the demand curve

Consumers seek to maximise total satisfaction (utility) derived from scarce resources (disposable income). A fall in price increases the value for money of the product because it increases the satisfaction per £ spent upon it compared to that available from other goods (assuming the prices of those goods are unchanged). The demand for the good whose price has fallen will increase, with demand for other goods falling. This is called the **substitution effect**.

 **BPP**

2.4 Conditions of the demand curve

A demand curve is drawn on the assumption of 'all other things being equal', ie on the assumption that, apart from price, there are no other potential influences on demand change in the current time period.

However, there are other factors which can influence demand, and these are sometimes called the **conditions of demand**. Here are some examples:

- Level of **disposable income** (income after tax):
  - **A normal good** is one where buyers buy more as their income increases.
  - **An inferior good** is one where buyers buy **less** as their income increases.
  - **A necessity good** is one where buyers continue to buy regardless of changes to their income levels.
- Price of **substitute goods** (two or more goods that satisfy the same need; for example, tea and coffee)
- Price of **complementary goods** (two or more goods that are consumed together; for example, tea and milk)
- The pattern of **tastes and preferences** for the product
- **Market expectations** of future changes in the price of the good (or shortages of it)

If there is a **change in the conditions of demand** then the demand curve will **shift** to the left or right.

Illustration 2: Mini cars continued

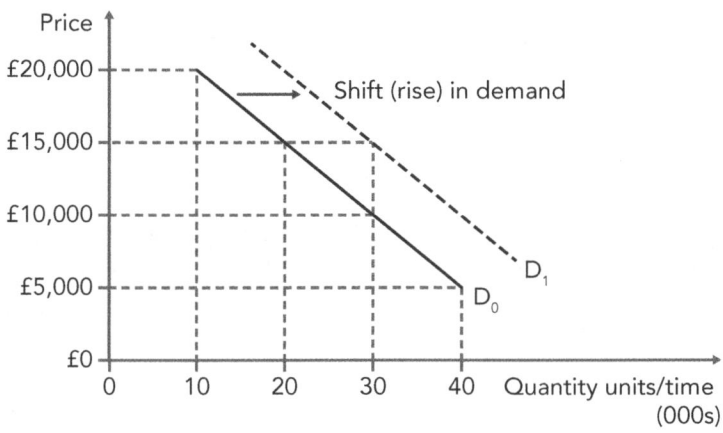

The demand curve has shifted outwards (from D_0 to D_1).

This could be caused by, for example, an increase in consumers' disposable income.

Activity 2: Law of demand

Explain how each of the following conditions of demand might lead the demand curve for Mini cars to shift to the left (inwards)?

Action	Explain impact on demand
Price of substitutes	
Price of complements	
Pattern of tastes and preferences	
Market expectations	

3 Micro-economic environment – supply

3.1 Supply

Supply is the amount (quantity) which firms are willing and able to supply to the market at a given price over a certain time period.

The law of supply: As the price of a good rises, all other things being equal, the quantity supplied of that good increases.

The relationship between price and quantity supplied can be illustrated as a **supply curve**; this shows the minimum prices necessary to encourage firms to supply a given quantity of a product or service.

 Illustration 3: Supply curve

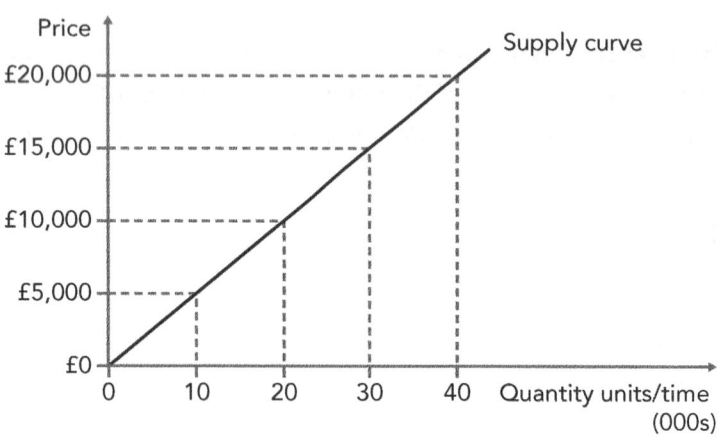

The diagram shows the supply of Mini cars.

Price/unit (£)	Quantitity supplied (No. of Minis pa)
5,000	10,000
10,000	20,000
15,000	30,000
20,000	40,000

A supply curve can represent a single firm (as here) or the whole market.

The supply curve slopes upwards from left to right, reflecting a direct relationship between price and quantity (ie as price rises, quantity supplied rises).

(a) **Extension of supply**: Increase in quantity supplied because price has risen. Shown by a rightward movement **along** the existing curve.

(b) **Contraction of supply**: Decrease in quantity supplied because price has fallen. Shown by a leftward movement **along** the existing curve.

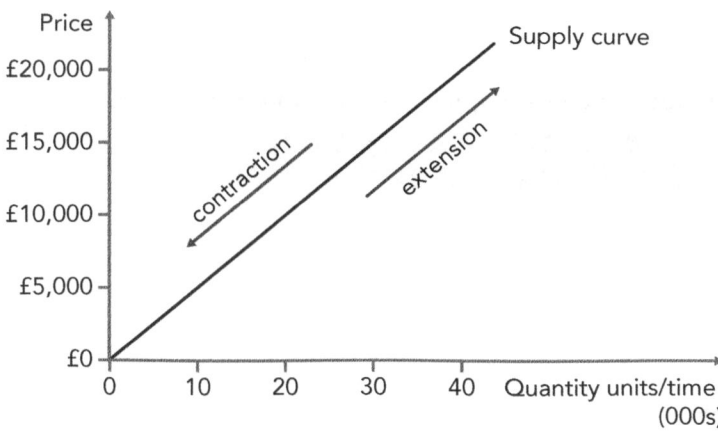

3.2 Explanation of supply curve

Profit is the difference between total revenue and total cost. A rise in market price, all other things being equal, increases the profit available from the product and so firms will want to produce more of it ie they will supply more of the product whose price has increased, by transferring more resources into making that product instead of making alternative products whose prices have stayed constant.

3.3 Conditions of the supply curve

A supply curve is drawn on the assumption of 'all other things being equal', ie that, apart from price, no other influences on supply are changing.

However, there could be other influences on supply and these are sometimes called the **conditions of supply**. Here are some examples:

- The **costs of production** (eg cost of labour)
- The **availability** of productive resources (affects amount available)
- Level of **indirect taxes** (eg a tax on the supply of petrol) or **subsidies**
- Prices of **substitutes in production** (alternative products which the firm could produce)
- Prices of **complements in production**: where goods are by-products of each other (eg sheep milk and wool)

If there is a **change in the conditions of supply** then the supply curve will **shift** to the left or right.

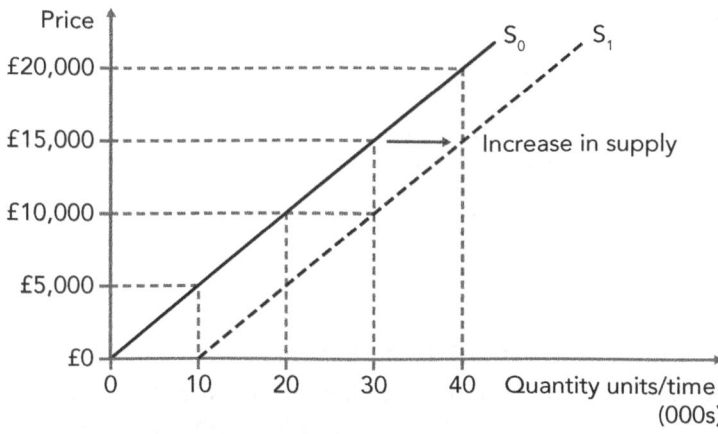

The supply curve has shifted outwards, from S_0 to S_1. This could be caused by, for example, a fall in production costs.

Activity 3: Law of supply

Forecast the effect of the following factors on the supply curve of wheat in Europe.

Action	Explain impact on supply
A poor growing season	
A rise in the cost of farm labour	
A rise in the price available for oats (an alternative crop)	
Government scheme to pay £1 per tonne subsidy to wheat farmers	

4 Micro-economic environment – price

4.1 Equilibrium price

Prices will be determined by the relationship between supply and demand.

Equilibrium price: The price at which quantity demanded and quantity supplied will be equal, and which will be restored by market forces following any changes in the conditions of either supply or demand.

Illustration 4: Mini cars continued from Illustrations 1 and 2

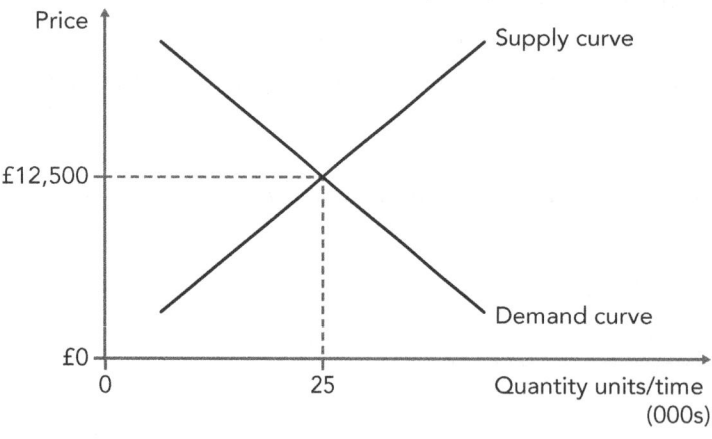

4.2 Movement to equilibrium

The market mechanism operates to remove situations of disequilibrium:

- **Shortage:** where quantity demanded exceeds quantity supplied at the prevailing market price (ie there is excess demand). This will encourage suppliers to make more goods as the price will rise making additional production more profitable. Where demand is above supply, consumers will find it hard to find supplies of the product. Firms will see a rise in sales. As a result firms will increase prices and extend supply by transferring resources to this product to get higher profits. As price rises, demand contracts as consumers find substitutes giving better value for money. This will continue until the shortage is eliminated.

- **Surplus:** where quantity supplied exceeds quantity demanded at the prevailing market price (ie there is excess supply). Where supply is above demand, firms will see a rise in unsold products

(inventory). As a result firms will cut prices and supply. As price falls, demand extends as consumers are attracted by the fall in price.

4.3 Functions of the price mechanism

The role of the price of the product in removing shortages and surpluses is sometimes referred to as the **price mechanism**.

The price mechanism has three functions:

- **Signalling** to producers where supply is too low (shortages) or too high (surpluses)
- **Rationing and allocating** the resources of a firm to produce those goods that are in high demand
- **Rewarding** firms for meeting consumer needs

4.4 Competition

The level of competition in any micro-economic environment will be influenced by:

- **Product features** – More modern products will shift demand patterns, allowing innovative and fashionable products to be sold at higher prices.
- **The number of sellers and buyers** – As seen in this section, any imbalance between supply and demand will cause an industry to become more or less competitive depending on the level of profits than can be earned.
- **Barriers to entry** – Where these exist it prevents new entrants into a market restricting supply eg new drugs are patent protected meaning that the inventor can operate a monopoly supply for the life of the patent.
- **Location** – If goods or services are affected by local supply/demand conditions then the local equilibrium price and profits may fluctuate, eg identical goods may sell at different prices in different markets.
- **Availability of information** – If buyers have information about availability and prices they can shop around, reducing the power of suppliers.

5 Sustainability

Sustainability encourages an organisation to focus on the creation of long-term consumer and employee value.

Sustainability is often evidenced by the implementation of **'green' strategies**.

However, sustainability doesn't relate only to environmental issues. In reality the challenge for businesses is to simultaneously deliver:

- **Social justice** – being a good corporate citizen. This can be evidenced by good employment practices.
- **Environmental quality** – striving to be environmentally neutral, eg planting trees to offset wood used in the production process.
- **Economic prosperity** – creating and sharing the economic wealth generated, eg shunning aggressive tax avoidance schemes, instead choosing to pay your 'fair share' of tax on your corporate profits.

Pursuing these aims will require organisations to build sustainability measures into their corporate reporting structures. If organisations focus too much on short-term issues at the expense of the longer term, this could damage their longer-term reputation and prospects.

Illustration 5: Sustainability reporting

Virat runs an energy-intensive manufacturing plant in Asia. All of his clients are based in North America and Europe, where some companies are keen to off-shore polluting and energy-intensive processes in order to make themselves appear more 'green' in the eyes of their customers.

Analysis

There are two issues here:

(a) Virat's business needs to look at its own sustainability record. If their activities are polluting as well as energy intensive he needs to consider how any pollution can be reduced/eliminated or offset. Virat's business should aim to leave its environment in the condition in which it found it. In terms of energy usage Virat should look to see if energy-efficient measures can be implemented in his factory (energy-efficient lighting etc), or whether it is possible to source renewable energy such as wind or solar power – perhaps solar panels could be installed onto the roof of his factory?

(b) Some of Virat's clients are 'greenwashing'. This means they are pretending to have sustainable processes, when in fact they have unsustainable supply chains. These companies need to be transparent about how their products are made and the true cost to the environment of making and transporting the goods that they sell.

5.1 The challenges of being sustainable

There is near-universal acceptance of the need to act sustainably in business. However, achieving sustainable process is difficult for a number of reasons.

- **Long-term vs short-term views** – The concept of sustainability is based on the ethos of preserving resources for future generations. Companies however are judged on their shortterm success, eg profit/dividends/tax yield. As such it is hard to balance a long-term outlook with the need to deliver short-term financial objectives demanded by key stakeholders.

- **Stakeholder views** – As seen in an earlier chapter, stakeholder management is a complex and tricky process. Quite simply, acting sustainably may not be in the interests of some influential stakeholders, and without the support of shareholders and lenders companies may be unable to invest in the sustainable projects desired by less influential stakeholder groups.

- **Resource management** – In manufacturing there is increasing awareness of the rarity of certain minerals. If these are used up faster than they can be mined or recycled, then a company is reducing its long-term viability.

- **Holistic impact** – Any organisation that attempts to convert to a 100% sustainable business needs to be aware of the far-reaching impacts. These will include, but not be limited to:

  - Effect on products and services – switching to sustainable ingredients can affect the quality the goods being made

  - Impact on customers – some sustainability actions increase costs, are customers prepared to pay for more sustainable products and services?

  - Employees – if products/services/process need to change then employees will need to be retrained

  - Workplace – any changes to processes may impact on how people work, this can cause some cultural impacts. These could be positive ('I'm proud work for a more sustainable company') or negative ('Why are we wasting money on all these changes when I'm not getting a big pay rise?').

  - Supply chain – can our current suppliers adapt to our new sustainability processes, or do we need to find new suppliers?

  - Business functions and processes – changing the way products and services are made/delivered may require an organisation to completely rethink how the work is done. This could result in new structures, machinery, software etc.

Accountants have a 'public interest' duty, and this will include ensuring that any sustainability reporting that a company presents is fair and accurate. The finance function will therefore need to audit any sustainability measures included in the financial statements, to ensure that they represent a 'true and fair view' in the same way as the traditional aspects of the financial statements, such as the Statement of Financial Position and Statement of Profit or Loss.

Chapter summary

- PESTLE analysis is used by organisations to analyse their macro-economic environment to scan for threats and opportunities, and monitor how these change over time.
- Demand is the amount or quantity of a certain good that the market will buy at a given price.
- The law of demand states that ss the price of a good falls, all other things being equal, the quantity demanded of that good increases.
- Demand is impacted by levels of disposable income, substitutes, complements, tastes and preferences and market expectations.
- Supply is the amount (quantity) which firms are willing and able to supply to the market at a given price over a certain time period.
- Prices will be set by the interaction between supply and demand.
- The equilibrium price is the price at which quantity demanded and quantity supplied will be equal, and which will be restored by market forces following any changes in the conditions of either supply or demand.
- Shortages and surpluses are removed by the price mechanism.
- Sustainability refers to the need for organisations to operate in a manner which means they can continue to operate over the longer term.
- Sustainability can be measured with reference to social justice, environmental quality and economic prosperity.

Activity answers

Activity 1: PESTLE analysis

	Threat – identify briefly	Action to reduce the threat – explain what the University can do
Social	**Lack of work-place skills** – this may discourage people from going to university if they do not feel they will get a job after graduating.	Discuss with employers the skills that graduates are lacking and incorporate these into the University's courses.
Economic	**Cost of degrees increasing** – this may reduce demand for courses.	The University could offer bursaries to reduce the cost to its most financially disadvantaged graduates.
Technological	**Lack of online course capability** – potential graduates could be lost to other universities with a better online offering.	Invest in the infrastructure needed eg hardware, software and staff training and course design.

Please note, you would not need the detailed explanations we have provided here.

Activity 2: Law of demand

Action	Explain impact on demand
Price of substitutes	Price of substitutes: fall in price of another compact saloon (eg Beetle) making the alternative relatively more attractive than a Mini.
Price of complements	Price of complements: rise in insurance premiums on Minis.
Pattern of tastes and preferences	Tastes and preferences: Minis cease to be fashionable.
Market expectations	Expectations: Mini prices expected to fall due to more competition between dealers. (Therefore, rather than buying a Mini now, a consumer will wait and buy one at a later date once the price is lower).

Activity 3: Law of supply

Action	Explain impact on supply
A poor growing season	Fall in supply (less available) – supply curve shifts to the left.
A rise in the cost of farm labour	Fall in supply (as labour costs rise, the amount of profit farmers can make from selling at any given price will fall) – supply curve shifts to the left.

Action	Explain impact on supply
A rise in the price available for oats (an alternative crop)	Fall in supply (produce oats instead of wheat) – supply curve shifts to the left.
Government scheme to pay £1 per tonne subsidy to wheat farmers	Rise in supply (more produced to get more subsidy) – supply curve shifts to the right.

Test your learning

1 **Match the factors to the correct aspect of a PESTLE analysis**

Factor	Element of PESTLE
Unemployment levels	▼
Changes in disposable income	▼
Sustainability	▼
Trade regulations	▼

Picklist

- Economic
- Environmental
- Legal
- Political
- Social
- Technological

2 **Complete this sentence:**

The law of [▼] : As the price of a good falls, all other things being equal, the

quantity demanded of that good [▼] .

Picklist

- Decreases
- Demand
- Increases
- Supply

3 **Which of the following will see demand increase as incomes fall?**

	✓
Normal goods	
Superior goods	
Substitutes	
Inferior goods	

4 **Describe the law of supply.**

5 **Describe THREE challenges that a company may need to overcome in order to implement sustainable policies.**

 BPP

4 Professional ethics for accountants

Learning outcomes

3.1 **The relevance of the ethical code for professional accountants**
Learners need to understand:

3.1.1 The principle of integrity:
- The effect of accountants being associated with misleading information
- The key ethical values of honesty, transparency and fairness when liaising with clients, suppliers and colleagues
- How integrity is threatened by self-interest and familiarity threats

3.1.2 The principle of objectivity:
- What is meant by a conflict of interest, including self-interest threats arising from financial interests, and compensation and incentives linked to financial reporting and decision making
- The importance of appearing to be objective as well as actually being objective
- The importance of professional scepticism when exercising professional judgement in relation to financial accounting and the link between compromised objectivity and possible accusations of bribery or fraud

3.1.3 The principle of professional behaviour:
- How compliance with relevant laws and regulations in relation to financial accounting is a minimum requirement but an act that is permitted by the law or regulations is not necessarily ethical
- The link between bringing disrepute on the profession and disciplinary action brought by a professional accountancy body

3.1.4 The principle of professional competence and acting with due care:
- How professional qualifications and continuing professional development (CPD) support professional competence

3.1.5 The principle of confidentiality:
- How financial accounting information confidentiality may be affected by compliance with data protection laws

3.1.6 Professional scepticism:
- The meaning of professional scepticism: assessing information critically, with a questioning mind, and being alert to possible misstatements due to error or fraud

		• The importance of professional scepticism when exercising professional judgement in relation to transactions recording and financial reporting
	3.1.7	The difference between a principles-based approach and a rules-based approach
	3.1.8	How documented organisational policies on relevant issues can be used as safeguards to prevent threats and ethical conflict from arising
	3.1.9	The types of safeguard that may be applied
	3.1.10	What an accountant should do when a threat cannot be eliminated or reduced to an acceptable level

Learners need to be able to:

	3.1.11	Recognise threats to integrity in financial accounting: intimidation/self-interest threats to present misleading information to users of financial statements
	3.1.12	Recognise threats to objectivity: intimidation, self-review, advocacy, self-interest, familiarity threats resulting in bias
	3.1.13	Recognise professional competence and due care threats: keeping knowledge up to date, pressure in working role, self-interest, self-review, familiarity threats
	3.1.14	Recognise areas in which up to date technical knowledge can be critical and the consequences of not maintaining CPD
	3.1.15	Recognise when confidential information: can or must be disclosed, when it must not be disclosed, and when situations pose a threat to confidentiality
	3.1.16	Recognise situations when professional scepticism should be applied and the action to be taken
	3.1.17	Recognise which safeguards may be appropriate

Assessment context

In your assessment you will be asked to demonstrate that you have a clear understanding of the ethical code of the AAT. Alongside this you must be able to recognise the main threats to good ethics, and be able to describe suitable safeguards against these.

Qualification context

At Level 2 in *The Business Environment* you learned about 'The fundamental principles of ethics for accounting technicians'.

At Level 4 in Internal *Accounting Systems and Controls* you will learn about 'the importance of ethics and sustainability within the accounting function'. In *Audit and Assurance* you will learn to 'Demonstrate the importance of professional ethics'.

Business context

Accountants owe a duty of care not only to their clients and employers, but also to their institutes, the wider accounting profession and also society at large. Given this broad and heavy burden the AAT, alongside all of the other accounting bodies, provide guidance to their members via their Code of Ethics. This code follows the 'principles-based approach', meaning that where explicit guidance is not provided the accountant must follow the spirit of the code.

Chapter overview

Professional ethics for accountants

AAT's Code of Ethics

- Objectivity
- Professional competence
- Professional behaviour
  - Threats
  - Safeguards
- Integrity
- Confidentiality

 **BPP**

Introduction

Accountants are in a position of trust, with their clients (to whom they provide accountancy and tax advice), employers (for whom they work) and the wider public. People that read financial statements, budgets and management accounts expect them to be accurate and objective. As such it is vital that accountants conduct themselves in a manner which upholds this trust. This will ensure that each accountant protects their own reputation, as well as the reputation of the profession as a whole.

> ### Assessment focus point
>
> Exam questions will likely focus on three aspects:
>
> (a) Identifying relevant ethical principles – the five fundamental principles
> (b) Explaining the actions that can be taken to combat ethical threats
> (c) Explaining the difference between principles- and rules-based approaches to ethics

1 AAT's Code of Ethics

Professional institutions such as AAT have an overriding duty to protect the public interest. To ensure their members act in a manner which achieves this they have developed codes of conduct to guide members' behaviour.

The **AAT Code of Ethics for Professional Accountants** (AAT, 2017) approved by International Ethics Standards Board for Accountants (IESBA) came into force on 1 January 2011. The Code was revised in 2017, and approved by AAT Council, to come into force on 15 July 2017.

AAT is a full member of **IFAC**. The mission of IFAC, as set out in its constitution, is 'the worldwide development and enhancement of an accountancy profession with harmonised standards, able to provide services of consistently high quality in the public interest'.

AAT's Code of Ethics is a principles-based documents providing **three areas of guidance**.

(a) It sets out the **five fundamental principles**.
(b) It provides a **conceptual framework** which members must apply to enable them to identify and evaluate threats to compliance with the fundamental principles and to respond appropriately to them.
(c) It provides **guidance and illustrations** on how to apply the conceptual framework in practice both generally and in specific problem situations.

1.1 Principle vs rules-based approaches

The AAT Code is a **principles-based approach**. That is to say it provides a framework of guided principles, which illustrate best practice. This approach is more flexible than the rules-based approach as it allows accountants to be guided by the principles rather than evaluating whether a specific rule has been broken. This means the accountant is bound to 'do the right thing' even where it is not clear that their actions could be viewed as a technical breach of a 'rule'.

The advantages and disadvantages of the principles-based approach are:

Advantages	Disadvantages
Flexibility to deal with complex situations	Can lead to subjective interpretations of guidelines
Illustrates the guiding principles	Potential for inconsistent actions
No loopholes to exploit	Guidelines can become de-facto rules

A **rules-based approach** would stipulate the strict rules, which, if broken would result in an ethical breach being identified. The advantages and disadvantages of the rules-based approach are:

Advantages	Disadvantages
Specific rules can be developed for specific situations	Where a rule does not exist a loophole can be exploited
Consistent application of rules	It's not possible to have a rule for every situation
Breaches are clear and easy to identify	Ethics is not always a black and white area

1.2 Five fundamental principles

KEY
TERM

Objectivity: The ability to make judgements and decisions **free from bias**. Within this the guidelines also make it clear that you are expected to avoid situations that cause a **conflict of interest** to arise.

Professional competence and due care: An accountant should only take on tasks which they are **technically competent** to perform. There is also a duty to **take reasonable care** and remain **technically up-to-date**.

Professional behaviour: Not doing anything that will discredit AAT or the wider accounting profession. This is defined as 'actions which a reasonable and informed third party, having knowledge of all relevant information, would conclude negatively affects the good reputation of the profession'.

Integrity: An individual should act in a manner that is **honest** and **straightforward** in all professional and business relationships. This extends beyond the work that an accountant produces and extends to the manner in which they **conduct** themselves.

Confidentiality: There is a duty to safeguard any information in your possession unless there is a legal or professional duty to disclose. This is an area that strays from ethics into law and in order to bring clarity to this area, AAT has provided a list of examples where confidential information can be disclosed:

(a)   When permitted by law

(b)   When permitted by the client or employer

(c)   When required by law

(d)   When permitted by a professional duty or right

There are a number of practical considerations to consider when applying these fundamental principles.

Fundamental principle	Practical considerations
Objectivity	Ensure professional decisions and judgements are not affected by bias or conflict of interest. You must take steps in professional and business relationships to protect objectivity. This can done by applying professional scepticism at all times eg not taking information at face value, being prepared to question its provenance. It is important not only to act objectively, but also to be seen to be acting objectively in the eyes of others.
Professional competence and due care	Ensure professional knowledge and skills are sufficient to meet the needs of clients by attaining and then retaining them through continuing professional development (CPD). Follow all professional and technical standards when performing services. Make clients aware of any limitations on service provision when performing professional services.

Fundamental principle	Practical considerations
Professional behaviour	Ensure compliance with all laws and regulations. Treat others with courtesy and consideration. Avoid discrediting fellow professionals in marketing campaigns. Unprofessional behaviour can result in disciplinary action from the AAT where it brings the accountancy profession into disrepute.
Integrity	Ensure fair dealing and truthfulness at all times. Being straightforward and honest in all professional and business relationships eg with clients, supplier and colleagues. Avoid any association with: • Materially false or misleading statements • Statements that are made recklessly • Statements that are based on incomplete information
Confidentiality	Information obtained in a business relationship should not be disclosed unless: • Disclosure is permitted by law and there is proper and specific authority from the client (such as the Data Protection Act allowing disclosure of personal information if the individual has consented to it) • Disclosure is required by the law (such as certain documents being required to be submitted as part of legal proceedings) • There is a professional right or duty to disclose if not prohibited by law (such as to comply with technical standards, a quality review into the firm or responding to an investigation by a body such as AAT) Confidential information should not be used to obtain personal advantage.

Illustration 1: Breach of AAT code

Samantha is the group accountant working for the Whizz Formula 1 team. Having been offered a job by a rival team, Samantha downloaded some sensitive technical data from the Whizz servers whilst working her notice period. When Whizz noticed similarities between their own car and that of Samantha's new team, they reviewed their server records and discovered the precise time of the data leak. Whilst they suspect Samantha took the data, they are unable to prove anything as Samantha had logged into someone else's machine and used her boss's passwords.

Analysis

In this case Samantha has committed several breaches of the AAT code. Quite obviously she has breached the confidentiality clause, but aside from this, she has demonstrated a lack of objectivity by placing herself in a conflict of interest. Stealing data also shows a lack of professional behaviour as well as a lack of integrity.

Activity 1: Donald

Donald's company is moving offices. During the move he finds his computer (which contains the payroll budgets) has been moved and he will not have access to it for a couple of days. The HR Director has requested information from the budgets for an important meeting today. Donald thinks he can remember the information but is not 100% sure of it.

Required

What should Donald do?

	✓
Politely refuse to provide the information.	
Provide the information from memory.	
Provide the information with a disclaimer on its accuracy.	
Make an educated guess and provide an update later.	

2 Threat and safeguards

The **conceptual framework** approach recognises threats to compliance with the fundamental principles and that it is impossible to identify all threats and appropriate mitigating action. Therefore, accountants are required to identify, evaluate and address significant threats using their best judgement and the fundamental principles as and when they occur. A useful tool in combating ethical threats is to apply professional scepticism in dealing with information provided by others.

KEY
TERM

Professional scepticism: An attitude that includes a questioning mind, being alert to conditions which may indicate possible misstatement due to error or fraud, and a critical assessment of evidence.

2.1 Threats

AAT's Code identifies five groups of **threats to fundamental principles** and provides safeguards that a professional accountant can apply to resolve them.

The groups of threats to professional ethics have been identified as:

- **Self-interest** – the threat that a financial/other interest will inappropriately influence the accountant's judgment or behaviour, eg an accountant recommends purchasing goods from Company X, who have just offered the accountant an expensive all expenses paid holiday.

- **Self-review** – the threat that a professional accountant will not appropriately evaluate the results of a previous judgment made, by themselves or a fellow accountant. This represents a threat to **integrity** and **objectivity**, eg an accountant should not review a report they prepared themselves.

- **Advocacy** – the threat that a professional accountant will promote a client's or employer's position to the point that the professional accountant's objectivity is compromised, eg an accountant may recommend buying parts from their partner's company even though better and cheaper parts can be purchased elsewhere.

- **Familiarity** – the threat that due to a long or close relationship with a client or employer, a professional accountant will be too sympathetic to their interests. This represents a threat to **integrity**, eg the accountant covers up mistakes made by a friend.

- **Intimidation** – the threat that a professional accountant will be deterred from acting objectively because of actual or perceived pressures, including attempts to exercise undue influence over the professional accountant, eg an accountant threatens to sack a junior colleague who uncovers a fraud/error.

To help overcome these threats, the Code suggests that the accountant should:

- **Eliminate the circumstances** (including interests and relationships) that created the threat
- **Apply safeguards** to reduce the level of the threat
- **Decline** or **end the professional activity**

2.2 Safeguards

In terms of **safeguards** these could include:

- Education, training and experience requirements
- Corporate governance requirements
- Duty to report breaches of ethics requirements
- Professional or regulatory monitoring and disciplinary procedures
- Effective complaint systems that enable professional accountants and the public to draw attention to unethical behaviour

The following safeguards may also be found in the work environment:

- Corporate oversight, organisational systems and internal controls
- Organisational ethics and codes of conduct (policies and procedures)
- Recruitment procedures to identify high calibre staff and subsequent training and education on organisational policies and procedures
- Employee performance and management systems and policies
- Communication channels to encourage employees to report ethical concerns to the senior leadership without fear

The following table provides some examples of ethical threats, and examples of safeguards that might mitigate those threats.

Ethical threat	Safeguard
Employer requesting the accountant to disregard accounting standards	Obtain professional or legal advice on the matter. Use the employer's formal dispute resolution process.
Employer requesting the accountant to undertake work that they are not trained sufficiently for, or, not providing enough time to produce the work diligently	Request additional training or time. Obtain assistance from those with sufficient training.
Accountant being offered an inducement (such as cash or a gift) to break their ethical responsibilities	Turn down the inducement. Report to appropriate parties (such as superiors or the professional body after taking legal advice).
Accountant being pressured to offer an inducement to another	Do not offer the inducement. Report the matter to appropriate parties.
Accountant under pressure to disclose confidential information as part of an outside investigate	Disclose the information in accordance with the statutory requirements.

The Code accepts that it may not be possible to mitigate all threats. Accountants are therefore expected to reduce threats to an 'acceptable level'. This means that a professional accountant using the 'informed third party' test would likely conclude that the accountant complies with the fundamental principles.

Activity 2: Ethical threats

Which of the following is a threat to the ethics of an accountant?

	✓
The UK Code of Corporate Governance	
Attendance at CPD courses	
External review	
Familiarity	

Chapter summary

The AAT's principles-based approach to ethics give the fundamental principles that members should follow in their professional lives. The principles are consistent with the IFAC code including:

- Objectivity
- Professional competence and due care
- Professional behaviour
- Integrity
- Confidentiality

The threats to ethics are:

- Self-interest
- Self-review
- Advocacy
- Familiarity
- Intimidation

Actions to safeguard against threats include:

- Exercise of professional scepticism
- Education, training and experience requirements
- Corporate governance requirements
- Duty to report breaches of ethics
- Effective complaint systems

Activity answers

Activity 1: Donald

The correct answer is:

	✓
Politely refuse to provide the information.	✓
Provide the information from memory.	
Provide the information with a disclaimer on its accuracy.	
Make an educated guess and provide an update later.	

Donald should not make himself party to inaccurate information. Options B and C potentially make him party to such misinformation. Option D could mean him breaking the principle of due care by rushing a calculation.

Activity 2: Ethical threats

The correct answer is:

	✓
The UK Code of Corporate Governance	
Attendance at CPD courses	
External review	
Familiarity	✓

Familiarity is one of the five threats to ethics.

Test your learning

1 **Complete the sentence:**

The AAT's Code of Ethics provides [▼] which members must apply to enable them to identify and evaluate threats to compliance with the fundamental principles and to respond appropriately to them.

Picklist
- A conceptual framework
- A list of principles
- Guidance and illustrations

2 **Which TWO of the following are disadvantages of the principles-based approach to ethics.**

	✓
Potential for consistent actions	
Guidelines can become de-facto rules	
Potential for subjective interpretations	
Removes loopholes which can be exploited	

3 **Which of the following refers to the ability to make judgements and decision free from bias?**

	✓
Objectivity	
Professional behaviour	
Integrity	
Confidentiality	

4 **Describe the concept of professional scepticism.**

5 **Familiarity is likely to be a threat to which one of these ethical principles?**

	✓
Integrity	
Confidentiality	
Professional competence	
Professional behaviour	

 **BPP**

Ethical conflicts

Learning outcomes

3.2		**Ethical conflicts and reporting unethical behaviour**
		Learners need to understand:
	3.2.1	How ethical conflicts arise
	3.2.2	How to determine whether behaviour is ethical or unethical
	3.2.3	Key organisational values and compliance with regulations: • Being transparent with customers and suppliers • Reporting financial and regulatory information clearly and on time • Whether to accept and give gifts and hospitality • Paying suppliers a fair price and on time • Providing fair treatment, decent wages and good working conditions to employees • Use of social media
	3.2.4	The stages in the process for ethical conflict resolution when a situation presents a conflict in application of the fundamental principles
	3.2.5	What happens when a course of action is unethical: • When disciplinary action by the relevant professional accountancy body may be brought against the accountant for misconduct, and the possible penalties that can arise • When internal disciplinary procedures may be brought against the accountant by the employer for unethical or illegal behaviour
	3.2.6	The link between lack of professional competence and due care and claims for breach of contract and professional negligence
	3.2.7	The requirement for professional indemnity insurance
	3.2.8	When and how to report unethical behaviour to responsible persons at work, including: • When it is appropriate to report that a breach of the ethical code has taken place • Report in line with formal internal whistle-blowing or 'speak-out' procedures that may be available for reporting unethical behaviour • Seeking advice confidentially from relevant managers or helplines as appropriate

- Circumstances when there may be public interest disclosure protection available under statute for blowing the whistle externally in the public interest in relation to certain illegal or unethical acts by the employer
- Seek third-party advice before blowing the whistle externally.

3.3   Money laundering

Learners need to understand:

3.3.1   Money laundering law and regulations:
- The process of money laundering (layering, placement, integration)
- The consequences for an accountant of failing to act appropriately in response to money laundering, including the potential for the offences of 'tipping off' and 'failure to disclose'
- The consequences for any person of 'prejudicing an investigation'
- The nature of the protection given to accountants by protected disclosures and authorised disclosures under money laundering law and regulations
- All accountants will be regulated by their professional body or by HMRC

3.3.12   The importance of reporting suspected money laundering in accordance with regulations:
- Select the information that should be reported by an accountant making a required disclosure in either an internal report or a suspicious activity report regarding suspicions about money laundering
- Timescales for disclosure of suspected money laundering

Assessment context

In your assessment you will be asked to demonstrate that you have a clear understanding of the ethical code of the AAT. Within this you are obligated to act in a manner that is lawful, so in this regard you will also be examined on your understanding of the law regulating money laundering, and what action you and your firm should take if you have suspicions that money laundering is taking place via your firm.

Qualification context

At Level 2 in *The Business Environment* you learned about 'The fundamental principles of ethics for accounting technicians'.

At Level 4 in *Internal Accounting Systems and Controls* you will learn about 'the importance of ethics and sustainability within the accounting function'. In *Audit and Assurance* you will learn to 'Demonstrate the importance of professional ethics'.

Business context

Ethics is a business critical matter for all organisations. Corporate scandals can ruin a company's reputation, leading to large fines as well as loss of clients and contracts.

In respect of money laundering, as an accountant in business you will be working in a regulated profession. It is vital that you understand your personal obligations to act within the law in this area.

Chapter overview

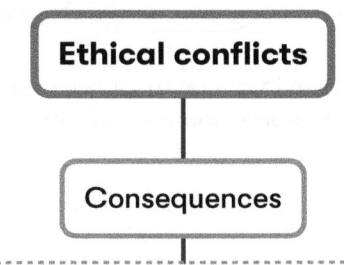

- The business
- The profession
- Identifying ethical conflicts
  - Resolving ethical conflicts
  - Money laundering
- Accountant
- Society

Introduction

From the previous chapter you are now aware of the ethical standards that accountants are judged against. In this chapter you will look at how ethical conflicts can occur, and best practice in dealing with these situations.

A particular ethical risk for accountants is the threat of being drawn into money laundering operations. It is essential therefore that you recognise the signs of money laundering, and what to do in the event that you suspect illegal activities are taking place.

Assessment focus point

Exam questions will likely focus on these aspects:

(a) Identifying ethical issues in a scenario

(b) Explaining the implications for accountants that act unethically

(c) Describing best practice in dealing with ethical conflicts

(d) Describing the elements of money laundering, and how to react should suspicious activities take place

1 Consequences of unethical behaviour

When considering the consequences of unethical behaviour it is sensible to start by considering the relationship between the AAT Code of Ethics and the law.

The AAT Code is a law of the association, and therefore any breach of the Code can give rise to disciplinary action. However the Code is not part of national law, and therefore will not automatically give rise to civil or criminal actions, though these could follow.

Illustration 1: Unethical behaviour

Frank is an AAT student working for Lennox Ltd. Frank has been put in charge of finalising construction contracts for a new warehouse and uses this position to negotiate some 'kickbacks' for himself with certain suppliers. In one instance, Frank agreed to accept a tender for building materials that was 10% higher than an equivalent quote of £500,000 on the understanding that Frank would receive an undeclared cash payment of half of the difference.

Analysis

In this instance, Frank has breached the AAT code with respect to objectivity, integrity, confidentiality and professional behaviour. He therefore faces disciplinary action from AAT that could result in his expulsion from the association. Aside from this, Frank's actions could lead to a criminal prosecution under the Bribery Act, so he faces prison and/or a fine; the undeclared payments may also lead to action from the tax authorities. Finally, Lennox Ltd would be justified in dismissing Frank, and could take civil action to recover any amounts they have overpaid as a result of the unlawful awarding of contracts.

The illustration above highlights the potential interaction between the AAT Code, the national law and an individual's employment contract.

When considering how AAT's Code, the law and contracts interact it is important to remember that the law overrides everything. As a student or member of AAT your secondary obligation is to AAT's Code, even if it may cause a breach of your employment, or other contract. Contracts such as an employment contract or ones entered into in the course of business are entered into voluntarily. This means that you always have a choice not to comply with a contractual obligation and you should do so if by complying with it you would break the law or be in breach of AAT's Code.

The consequences of unethical behaviour by organisations and their employees can be far reaching.

1.1 Accountants

An unethical accountant risks the following if their unethical behaviour is discovered:

- Being subject to a professional disciplinary hearing
- Being fined or being struck off as an accountant
- Losing their job, either through an employer disciplinary hearing or being unable to practice
- Their actions becoming public knowledge and their personal reputation damaged
- Being sued for damages by an affected party

1.2 The accountancy profession

Accountants have a high degree of trust placed on them by society. Therefore any high profile, or repeated breaches can have severe consequences for the whole profession. These may include:

- Loss of reputation
- Reduced employability of accountants
- Pressure by outside bodies to tighten up regulations and penalties
- Government intervention if it is thought the profession is incapable of self-regulation
- Accountancy bodies losing their 'chartered' status

1.3 Businesses

If a business knowingly acts unethically, or allows its employees to breach ethical codes, they face the following risks:

- Loss of reputation and therefore sales/contracts
- Threat of legal action or investigation by regulators
- Resignation of key ethically minded staff
- Business closure, resulting in redundancy

1.4 Society as a whole

Given that society relies upon the work of accountants to assess the profitability of organisations and their liability for tax, there are consequences for the wider society of unethical behaviour.

- The work of all accountants would be called into question.
- Unethical companies would eventually fail as they would lose public confidence.
- The financial markets would be affected if investors could not rely on audit reports and financial statements.
- The tax authorities may question tax computations, affecting the amount of tax collected.
- Criminals may gravitate towards the profession to make money from fraud or other financial crime.

 Illustration 2: Rogue trader

The notorious 'rogue trading' of Nick Leeson caused the collapse of Barings Bank in 1995 with debts of over £800m. Slack internal controls allowed Leeson to enter into a series of unhedged trades that went wrong, racking up huge losses that resulted in the world's oldest merchant bank being sold for a notional £1 to the Dutch Bank, ING. ING took on the Barings name, but little else.

Investors in Baring's lost millions, many employees lost their jobs and Leeson spent four years in a Singapore prison. In response to this, and other high-profile scandals, the UK started to review its corporate governance frameworks.

Activity 1: AAT Code of Ethics

Which of the following statements is correct?

	✓
The AAT Code of Ethics has the power of law.	
The AAT Code of Ethics is the law of AAT.	
Breaches of the AAT Code of Ethics are assessed in court.	
The AAT Code of Ethics differs from country to country.	

2 Identifying ethical conflicts

Ethical conflicts arise in situations where **two values or requirements seem to be incompatible.** They can also arise where two conflicting demands or obligations are placed on an individual.

Ethical conflicts can occur as a result of tensions between four sets of values:

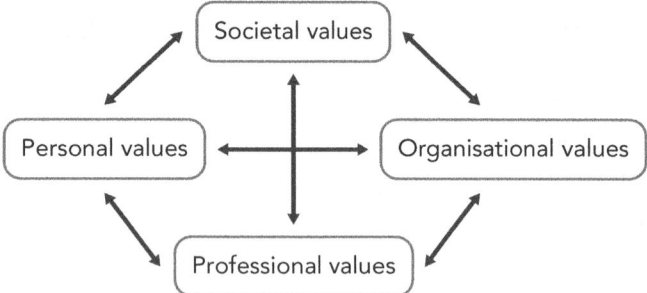

Societal values – the obligations imposed by national law and customs.

Personal values – the values and principles held by the individual. In the workplace this can include:

- Whether it is 'ok' to accept gifts/hospitality
- Use of social media

Organisational values – the values and principles of the organisation where the employee works, often laid down in a corporate ethical code. Additionally, organisations need to be mindful of:

- Being transparent with customers and suppliers
- Reporting financial and regulatory information clearly and on time
- Paying suppliers a fair price, and on time
- Fair treatment of staff, including those employed through the supply chain

Professional values – the values and principles of the professional body that the individual is a member of, again laid down in ethical codes.

Aside from these, contractual obligations can add an additional layer of complexity.

Illustration 3: Ethical values

Societal values and corporate values

An individual may be asked by their employer to act in an illegal way, for example, to discriminate against a disabled or ethnic minority employee.

Personal values and corporate values

An individual may not agree with certain activities of their organisation, such as the use of child labour in foreign factories. Whilst not necessarily illegal, it goes against their own moral beliefs.

Professional values and corporate values

An individual is put into a position by their employer where they are required to amend a set of accounts to improve the profit figure. Such amendments go against the code of conduct of their accountancy body.

Contractual obligations

An interim chief executive has a clause entitling them to 10% of the value of any savings they can make over a six-month period. Having clashed several times with a high-level manager, they could make that person redundant and receive cash to the value of 10% of the salary saved.

2.1 Ethical dilemmas

Ethical dilemmas often arise when the boundaries between right and wrong are unclear and/or there is a choice between a good choice or the least wrong choice.

An ethical dilemma is not about a choice between personal preferences or compromises and the law or professional standards. Accountants should avoid thinking about themselves personally when making ethical decisions.

Personal preferences and compromises include issues such as friendships, families, memberships of organisations, politics and other beliefs. There is a risk that these may colour an accountant's perception of the situation, but they should have no place in the decision of how to deal with it.

Ethical dilemmas are often centred around **conflicts of interest**. Conflicts of interest occur when an individual is faced with two competing demands. For example, if an accountant is responsible for calculating their organisation's annual profit, and they will receive a bonus based on the size of the profit, the accountant has a conflict between the professional duty to calculate an accurate and technically correct profit figure and the knowledge that a larger profit will earn them a bigger bonus.

When dealing with a conflict of interest, it is usually a good idea for the individual concerned to declare it or withdraw from the situation that is causing the conflict.

Other **practical examples** of ethical dilemmas arising include:

- Pressure from an overbearing colleague or from family or friends
- Members asked to act contrary to technical and/or professional standards
- Divided loyalties between colleagues and professional standards
- Publication of misleading information
- Members having to do work beyond their degree of expertise or the experience they possess
- Personal relationships with other employees or clients
- Gifts and hospitality being offered.

Activity 2: Values

Which of the following obligations are imposed by national laws?

	✓
Professional values	
Personal values	
Corporate values	
Societal values	

3 Resolving ethical dilemmas

AAT's Code (AAT, 2017) is clear – accountants should always respond to an ethical conflict. **Silence or inactivity** may in itself be a breach of the Code.

The general approach to **resolving ethical issues** is given by the following checklist.

(a) **Check all the relevant facts** – identify and document where possible. Do not rely on word of mouth.

(b) **Is it ethical?** – have all of the ethical issues been considered? Refer to the AAT Code of Ethics.

(c) **Identify any fundamental principlesengaged** – refer to the AAT Code.

(d) **Refer to internal ethical procedures** – what actions does your firm advise you to take?

(e) **Consider possible courses of action** – escalate internally, seek professional legal advice or contact professional body/regulator.

(f) **Seek professional/legal advice** – AAT's ethics helpline, beware of confidentiality/whistleblowing regulations.

(g) **Refuse to be associated with the conflict** – move departments, resign or seek legal advice.

When dealing with such matters, the organisation should try and ensure:

- **Transparency** – Do you feel comfortable about the decision made, are your actions justifiable?
- **Effect** – Have all affected parties been considered, all stakeholders considered?
- **Fairness** – Would a rational bystander consider the outcomes to be fair?

3.1 Reporting ethical breaches in the workplace

Reporting potential breaches of ethical guidelines can be a tricky area, as any whistleblowing could harm working relationships. A sensible approach to this may include:

Step 1 Be confident that a breach has taken place. Take reasonable steps to establish the facts.

Step 2 Following internal procedures. For instance is there a confidential reporting mechanism in place, do you know who the designated Money Laundering Officer is?

Step 3 If you are still uncertain you could seek confidential advice from senior colleagues.

Step 4 In exceptional circumstances you could make a public disclosure eg you could report to the police where your employer is acting illegally. **It is crucial that you seek independent legal advice** before disclosing externally as this may be a breach of your own duty of confidentiality to your employer.

Activity 3: Resolving conflict

What should a solution to an ethical conflict be?

	✓
Acceptable to the employer	
Authorised by AAT	
Expressly permitted in IFAC's ethical code	
Consistent with fundamental principles	

3.2 Disciplinary action

As an AAT student member you can be held accountable for any unethical actions by:

- **Your employer** – Unethical action such as accepting bribes could result in internal disciplinary action. This can ultimately result in termination of your employment.
- **The AAT** – Unethical action on your behalf can be reported to the AAT which could result in a Disciplinary Tribunal hearing. In these instances:

- You will be given 42 days' notice of a hearing
- Within 28 days of receiving notice you can submit a written statement in response
- A hearing will be held, where the accusations will need to be proven on the balance of probabilities
- The Tribunal will consider its finings and issue a ruling. If misconduct is found further submissions will be invited.
- If misconduct is upheld the following sanctions are available:
    - Expulsions
    - Suspension
    - Conditions imposed
    - Written reprimand
    - Fines
    - Students can be declared unfitness for full membership
    - Student membership withdrawn
- **The law –** Unethical action that is illegal, eg money laundering, bribery, can result in prosecution.

3.3 Professional negligence

Where the unethical behaviour is due to a lack of professional competence eg giving wrong advice, this can give rise to claims for compensation for professional negligence.

 Illustration 4: Professional negligence

Bob runs a small accountancy practice, and employs Vic, an AAT trainee as one of his accounting and tax assistants.

Whilst Bob was on holiday Vic replied to a tax query from a client, Ulrika. Vic assured Ulrika that a particular tax mitigation scheme was 'fool proof' and, having received this advice, Ulrika implemented the scheme.

Ulrika has now written to Bob's firm demanding £25,000 in compensation. This was because HMRC challenged the scheme and won. The tax tribunal ordered Ulrika to pay a penalty of £20,000 and awarded costs of £5,000 against her.

Analysis

On the facts it appears that Bob's firm, acting through Vic has given a client incorrect advice. As such the firm is deemed to have acted negligently as is liable to the client for the losses she has suffered.

As an employee Vic will not be personally liable. It will be Bob's firm, and in all likelihood their insurer who will pay the monies to Ulrika.

3.4 Professional indemnity insurance

Anyone who practises as an **AAT bookkeeper** or **AAT accountant** is essentially self-employed, and as such faces personal liability in the event that they act negligently. As such, licensed members of the AAT are required to take out professional indemnity insurance to ensure that they are adequately covered to meet any legal claims. The level of cover required is:

- **Sole traders** – higher of: 2.5 times the firm's gross fee income, or £50,000
- **Partnerships** – higher of: 2.5 times the firm's gross fee income, or £100,000
- **Limited companies** – higher of: 2.5 times the firm's gross fee income, or £100,000

 **BPP**

4 Money laundering

> **Money laundering:** The process by which the proceeds of crime, which have illegitimate origins, are converted into assets that appear to be legitimate.

4.1 Phases of money laundering

The process usually comprises of three distinct phases:

(a) **Placement** – the disposal of the proceeds of crime into an apparently legitimate business property or activity.

(b) **Layering** – the transfer of money from place to place, in order to conceal its criminal origins.

(c) **Integration** – the culmination of placement and layering, giving the money the appearance of being from a legitimate source.

4.2 Money laundering offences

Money laundering was first made a criminal offence in the UK under the Drug Trafficking Offences Act 1986, but is now regulated by the **Proceeds of Crime Act 2002** (HMSO 02), and The Money Laundering, Terrorist Financing and Transfer of Funds Regulations 2017 amongst others.

The Proceeds of Crime ACt 2002 has defined **three categories of offence**, these being:

(a) **Laundering** – the offences of concealing, disguising, converting, transferring, or removing criminal property from the UK.

(b) **Failure to report** – it is an offence for someone who knows or suspects that another person is engaged in money laundering not to report that fact to the appropriate authority. This offence only relates to individuals working in a regulated industry, eg accountants.

(c) **Tipping off** – it is an offence to make a disclosure likely to prejudice a money laundering offence already being undertaken, or which may be undertaken, eg alerting your client to the fact they are under investigation for laundering.

4.3 Penalties for money laundering

The penalties for those found guilty of money laundering are:

- **Laundering** – a maximum 14-year prison sentence is possible, and/or a fine. Additionally, the police may seize the illegitimate assets
- **Failure to report** – punishable by a maximum five-year sentence and/or a fine
- **Tipping off** – punishable by a maximum two-year sentence and/or a fine

4.4 Duties of accountants regarding money laundering

Typically accountants are bound by a duty of confidentiality to their clients. However, in the case of actual or suspected money laundering you are directed to:

- Report your suspicions/evidence to your firm's **Nominated Officer**, or **Money Laundering Reporting Officer** (MLRO)
- Where suspicion is upheld the MLRO must submit a **Suspicious Activity Report** (SAR) to the National Crime Agency as soon as it is 'reasonably practicable'

It is important that when internally reporting your suspicions of money laundering that this is made directly to the **MLRO**. Reporting to a colleague or your line manager is not sufficient to comply with the regulations around reporting.

A correctly made external SAR provides **full immunity** from action for any breach of confidentiality.

Activity 4: Luigi and Mario

Luigi works as a bookkeeper for a small accounting firm, and suspects that one of his most valuable clients, and best friends, Mario, is laundering money through his ice-cream parlour

business. Concerned that Mario could land himself in trouble after noticing that the tax authorities were starting to take a closer than normal look at the books of the ice-cream parlour Luigi emailed Mario saying:

'Mario, not sure if your ice-cream parlour is 100% legitimate, but I'd say for the foreseeable future you should stick to selling cones and lollies only, if you know what I mean.'

Required

Which TWO of the following offences has Luigi committed?

	✓
Money laundering	
Tipping off	
Bribery	
Failure to report	

Chapter summary

Unethical behaviour will have consequences for:

- You as an accountant
- The accountancy profession
- Society as a whole

Ethical conflicts are situations where two ethical values or requirements seem to be incompatible. They can also arise where two conflicting demands or obligations are placed upon you.

A conflict of interest arises where you have a duty to two or more parties. Whilst working information or other matters may arise that mean you cannot continue work for one party without harming another.

Ethical conflicts may rise from:

- Pressure from an overbearing colleague or from
- Being asked to act contrary to technical and/or professional standards
- Divided loyalties between colleagues and standards
- Publication of misleading information
- Having to do work beyond your degree of expertise/experience you possess
- Personal relationships with other employees or clients
- Gifts and hospitality being offered

Money laundering is a threat to all accountants. It consists of three processes:

- Placement
- Layering
- Integration

The three offences of money laundering are:

- Laundering
- Failing to report
- Tipping off

Suspicions of money laundering should be reported to the firm's Money Laundering Reporting Officer, who should submit a Suspicious Activity Report within a reasonably practicable period to the National Crime Agency.

Activity answers

Activity 1: AAT Code of Ethics

The correct answer is:

	✓
The AAT Code of Ethics has the power of law.	
The AAT Code of Ethics is the law of AAT.	✓
Breaches of the AAT Code of Ethics are assessed in court.	
The AAT Code of Ethics differs from country to country.	

AAT's code is not part of national law, and breaches are assessed internally, not in court. The Code is a global entity – there are no regional variants.

Activity 2: Values

The correct answer is:

	✓
Professional values	
Personal values	
Corporate values	
Societal values	✓

The obligations imposed by national law and customs.

Activity 3: Resolving conflict

The correct answer is:

	✓
Acceptable to the employer	
Authorised by AAT	
Expressly permitted in IFAC's ethical code	
Consistent with fundamental principles	✓

Any solution must be consistent with fundamental ethical principles. They do not have to be authorised by AAT or expressly permitted in IFAC's code. An ethical solution may be unacceptable to an employer who is behaving unethically.

Activity 4: Luigi and Mario

The correct answers are:

	✓
Money laundering	
Tipping off	✓
Bribery	
Failure to report	✓

Luigi suspected Mario of money laundering so should have reported this to the money laundering officer within his firm. He compounds this mistake by tipping Mario off, putting a potential criminal prosecution at risk.

Test your learning

1 Unethical behaviour by an accountant could have negative consequences for which of the following? SELECT ALL THAT APPLY.

	✓
Businesses	
The AAT	
The accounting profession	
The accountant	

2 Which THREE of the following are guidelines to organisations dealing with possible ethical breaches?

	✓
Transparent investigation	
Consider all parties affected	
Punishing wrong doers	
Cover-up to protect reputations	
Fairness in the process	

3 Complete the sentence:

If you are accused of acting unethically the AAT may call a Disciplinary Tribunal hearing. You will be given [   ] days' notice of such a meeting.

4 What level of professional indemnity insurance does an accountancy partnership need to take out?

	✓
Higher of 2.5 times gross fee income or £50,000	
Higher of 2.5 times gross fee income or £100,000	
£50,000	
£100,00	

5 Describe the potential penalties for accountants found guilty of money laundering offences.

BPP

Technology and data

Learning outcomes

4.1	**Technology**
	Learners need to understand:

4.1.1	The impact of emerging and developing technologies on accounting systems:
	• Automation of processes
	• AI and machine learning
	• Blockchain
	• Electronic filing of documents
	• Electronic signing of documents
	• Data analytics

4.1.2	How technological developments have increased outsourcing and offshoring, which has impacted business development:
	• Cost structure
	• Markets
	• Locations

4.1.3	The effect of automation and AI in accounting systems on the role of the accountant and the finance function

4.1.4	The key features of cloud accounting:
	• Access to data and information from anywhere
	• Remote data storage so no backup by the business is required
	• Automation capabilities
	• Availability of apps/plug-ins/add-ins
	• Interactions with stakeholders
	• Real-time data

4.1.5	Benefits and limitations of cloud accounting for an organisation

4.2	**Data protection, information-security and cybersecurity**
	Learners need to understand:

4.2.1	The principles of data protection:
	• Lawfulness, fairness, and transparency
	• Purpose limitation
	• Data minimisation

		• Accuracy
		• Storage limitation
		• Integrity and confidentiality (security)
		• Accountability
	4.2.2	The impact of data protection breaches on the individual and business
	4.2.3	The importance of maintaining information security: • Accounting systems access levels • Security controls, ie firewalls • Integrity controls (input, processing, and output controls)
	4.2.4	The importance of cybersecurity to address cyber risks
	4.2.5	The risks to data and operations posed by cyberattacks
5.1		**Information requirements in a business organisation** Learners need to understand:
	5.1.1	The attributes of good quality information
	5.1.2	The type, purpose, and characteristics of information at operational, managerial and corporate/strategic levels within an organisation
	5.1.3	The characteristics of big data: • Value • Variety • Velocity • Veracity • Volume
	5.1.4	The sources of internal and external big data
	5.1.5	The sources of internal and external big data
	5.1.6	The need to apply professional scepticism in relation to big data
	5.1.7	The use of data analytics from external sources

Assessment context

Your assessment will examine how will you understand the various types of novel technologies that organisations can use to meet their informational needs. Alongside this you need to demonstrate that you understand the external threats to information systems, and how these can be managed.

Qualification context

At Level 2 in *The Business Environment* you learned about 'the importance of information to business operations'.At Level 4 in *Internal Accounting Systems and Controls* you will learn to 'Understand the impact of technology on accounting systems'.

Business context

Increasingly it is said that 'information is power'. Modern businesses need to build systems capable of rapid data collection, processes and analysis, often from their environments. This requires open systems, and thus exposes the business's system to cyber-attacks, which necessitates continual investment in cyber security to combat these threats.

Chapter overview

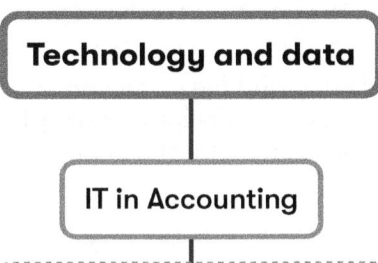

Technology and data

IT in Accounting

- Information
- Process automation
- Data protection
  - Seven principles
  - Processing data
  - Cyber risks
  - Cyber security
- Outsourcing and offshoring
- New technologies
  - Blockchain
  - AI
  - Big data
  - Cloud

Introduction

Technological change is a constant; as an accountant in business you must keep abreast of the latest developments so that your organisation can benefit from the gains that technology can deliver.

From an accountant's perspective the automation of data gathering and the extraction of information and intelligence from that that data presents massive opportunities for analysis. However, any entity that gathers, holds, and processes data must be mindful of complying with Data Protection laws.

Assessment focus point

Exam questions will likely focus on these aspects:

(a) Identifying the different types of technology that an organisation can deploy

(b) Explaining the advantages that different types of technology have

(c) Describing the data protection legal requirements, and the consequences for organisations that breach these

(d) Describing the cyber-attacks that organisations face, and the cyber-defences available to protect them

1 Information and technology in accounting

1.1 Information

A key role of the finance or accounting function is to deliver information for decision making purposes. This is done by:

(a) **Gathering** data (unstructured facts and figures)

(b) **Transforming** into information (something that has a value)

(c) **Analysing** for insight, using this information for the organisation's benefit.

1.2 Levels of information

In Chapter 2 you saw that management takes place at three different levels of the organisation:

The finance function sits at the middle level of the organisation and they will be responsible for ensuring that each level get the appropriate type of information they need for decision-making purposes.

Strategic level information will be largely:

- Unstructured – no consistent format
- Externally sourced
- Focused on the long-term strategy of the business

Management level information will be largely:

- Semi-structured
- Internally sourced, but with some information on market and competitors
- Focused on the success of existing strategic plans, structured around annual, six-monthly, or quarterly targets

Operational level information will be largely:

- Structured, eg sales and inventory reports
- Internally sourced
- Focused on the daily, weekly, or monthly operational processes

1.3 Characteristics of good quality information

Irrespective of which level of the organisation, **good quality information** will have the following characteristics:

- **A**ccurate – this means as accurate as the user requires.
- **C**ost-effective – it should not cost more to obtain the data than the value that can be driven from it.
- **C**omplete – all of the information that is required to make a decision should be presented.
- **U**nderstandable – in a format that the user can understand eg avoid technical jargon.
- **R**elevant – to the needs of the user eg operational manager need operational information.
- **A**ccessible – the user should be able to access the information where and when they need it.
- **T**imely – information should arrive on time eg before it is needed for a decision.
- **E**asy-to-use – presented in a medium appropriate to the user.

1.4 Process automation

> **Process automation:** The ability of systems to perform routine activities (such as the processing of data and assembling electronic components) without the input of a human.

Traditional process automation involves a machine carrying out a simple, repetitive task. Modern process automation has made processes more automated and focusses on complex business areas that were previously thought as beyond the scope of automation.

Robotic process automation is a technology that enables the automation of routine, clerical activities. The main impact on organisations of automation is the increased speed and efficiency of processes and reduced staff costs.

1.5 Blockchain

> **Blockchain:** A form of a distributed ledger system.
>
> **Distributed ledger technology:** A technology that allows organisations and individuals who are unconnected to share an agreed record of events, such as ownership of an asset.

Blockchain is one form of distributed ledger technology. It is a way of recording transactions in 'blocks' which are linked to one another and secured against being altered using cryptography, based on complex calculations. Any party who has owned the asset can view the previous transaction data, but this information is not necessarily otherwise shared or publicly available.

Key aspects of blockchain:

- Participants of a blockchain record transactions on an online network that is publicly available and distributed to everyone.
- Details of transactions are recorded by all participants. Transactions are only accepted once all participants have updated their ledgers to reflect them.
- Network computers verify the transaction to make sure the records have all been updated correctly. Once the validation work is complete, the transaction is authorised and added to the blockchain. This means that a single system cannot itself add new blocks to the chain.

- Blocks are connected to a blockchain using a cryptographic hash that is generated from the previous block. This means the chain cannot be broken and each block is preserved permanently. It is only possible to amend previous blocks if the subsequent blocks are altered first.

Illustration 1: Blockchain

An example of blockchain is the Everledger system used by the diamond industry. Everledger helps the diamond industry prevent fraud and the transfer of stolen goods. All diamonds have unique characteristics (similar to how humans have individual fingerprints). The Everledger system creates an identity for every diamond by recording these unique characteristics. Every time a diamond is bought or sold; the sale is recorded by the system on the Blockchain so that the diamond's ownership can be traced.

Analysis

The single distributed ledger creates a record for each diamond, ensuring that the authenticity of each stone in the system can be verified every time it changes hands.

1.6 Impacts of blockchain on the finance function

Blockchain may have the following impacts on the **finance function**:

- The security and traceability of transactions may impact how businesses record their dealings with third parties.
- Smart contracts can be created which are self-executing agreements that utilise cryptography, digital signatures, and secure completion.
- Bitcoin and other cryptocurrencies are not covered by accounting standards and decisions need to be made how to record them.
- They allow money to cross borders easily and seamlessly by avoiding traditional intermediaries such as banks.

1.7 Artificial Intelligence (AI)

> **Artificial intelligence:** The ability of a computer system to assist to perform cognitive tasks such as making business decisions, finding patterns in data, or helping solve problems.

A key impact of automation and artificial intelligence systems (collectively known as intelligent systems) is that they harness the ability of computers to learn, make decisions and perform actions based on those decisions. This reduces the need for human involvement in a number of business operations, reducing costs and introducing efficient processes that add more value.

Cognitive computing is a collective name for several technologies including artificial intelligence, machine learning and natural language programming. These technologies enable the automation of more complex tasks such as advanced data analytics and reporting writing.

Machine learning is a subset of artificial intelligence that involves code being developed and designed to replicate how the human brain works. It uses experience from past events, data, connections, and probability and applies it in future situations by detecting patterns and making recommendations of what to do. Such systems are also designed to learn from mistakes and not to repeat them in the future. This way, they adapt and improve their functions over time.

1.8 Impact of artificial intelligence on the finance function

Some examples of how AI can support the **finance function** include:

- Simple processes can be automated
- Improved fraud detection as systems can better understand 'normal' and 'abnormal' transactions
- Predictive models can help forecast costs and revenues

- Improved analysis of unstructured data in contacts and emails

Electronic signature and filing

It is increasingly common to apply electronic signatures to documents, such as contracts, and to be able to file documents electronically, such as company accounts. These innovations allow teams to work remotely, however, these systems are inherently prone to cyber-risk, eg if someone steals your log-in credentials can they sign and file documents on your behalf?

1.9 Big data and data analytics

Big data: The vast volumes of data which are captured from various sources, such as web browsing and the internet of things that can be analysed to reveal patterns or trends, especially relating to human behaviour or interactions.

Data analytics: The collection, management and analysis of large data sets with the objective of discovering useful information that an organisation can use for decision making.

The **main use of big data in organisations** is to identify trends that may exist in vast quantities of data in the pursuit of value creation. Historically, organisations have been restricted as to the amount of data that they can process due to the storage limitations of existing computer systems, but with the reduction in storage costs and the availability of cloud computing, even small and medium-sized organisations can collect and store huge amounts of data.

Once collected, data analytics is used to **identify relationships** and **patterns** in the data in order to assist decision making for improved organisational performance.

1.10 Sources of big data

Sources of big data include:
- Human interactions with social networks, search engines, online retailers etc
- Machines, such as smart devices with sensors (the internet of things)
- Open data sources, such as statistics published by the government and public services
- Closed data sources, such as marketing databases, where data has been processed by research organisations and is available for a fee

1.11 Characteristics of big data

Big data has **five characteristics**:
- **Volume** – the quantity of data that is available. Big data is available relatively easily and in large quantities.
- **Velocity** – the speed at which big data can be accessed by an organisation. Big data is often available to an organisation in real time rather than at intervals such as on a weekly or monthly basis.
- **Variety** – the different forms that big data can take. It is often unstructured and can take many forms including free text, images, and audio. This makes analysis more complex and also takes up more storage space.
- **Veracity** – the trustworthiness or accuracy of big data. Despite an organisation's best efforts, data sets will contain inaccuracies, bias, anomalies, and irrelevant 'noise'. Therefore as much as possible needs to be done to verify the data before it can be trusted as accurate. This may require the user to **apply professional scepticism to big data.**
- **Value** – the ability of big data to add value to an organisation. Big data can enable organisations to truly get to know their customers and to extract value from this knowledge or to monetise it. For example, big data may help organisations identify the most loyal customers, so marketing or other resources can be used in a more cost effective or efficient manner. The right products can be targeted at the right customers at the right time to maximise profitability.

1.12 Limitations and benefits of big data

These five Vs illustrate some of the **limitations** of big data, eg can it be processed quickly enough? Can it be stored? Can the variety be accommodated? Can it be trusted?

Assuming these limitations can be overcome significant benefits can result, including:

*   **Deeper insight and understanding** – Intelligent use of data can reveal patterns and insight into how a business operates and identify previously unknown issues.
*   **Improved performance** – The processing of data and the creation of relevant management information in real time can result in improvements to operations, decision making and resource utilisation.
*   **Better market segmentation** – The needs and wants of customer groups can be increasingly refined, leading to better personalisation and customisation of products and services.
*   **Faster decision making** – Real-time processing of data results in faster decisions and advantage over the competition
*   **Innovation** – Existing products can be improved through the organisation better understanding the aspects of the product that customers value the most.
*   **Better risk management** – Data analytics can support all aspects of risk management processes.

To have value to an organisation, data needs to have meaning. Data analytics creates this meaning by assembling, filtering, sorting, highlighting and finally presenting the data in useful forms.

1.13 Impacts of big data on organisations

Some key impacts that big data and data analytics have on organisations are summarised below.

*   **Decision making** – More data can give rise to more information to assist decision making.
*   **Risk** – These can be better understood with more information.
*   **Product development** – Deeper insight into customer needs and trends can lead to products that better suit the needs of target markets.
*   **Marketing** – More information on markets can lead to better market segmentation and more targeted advertising.
*   **Performance management** – Deeper levels of understanding of the organisation's performance may identify previously unknown causes for poor performance that can be rectified.

Illustration 2: Big data

Big data is becoming an increasingly common feature of sales and marketing functions. For example commonly used apps such as Amazon and Spotify use big data, data analytics and AI to analyse consumer habits which they then use to identify emerging trends.

Analysis

Amazon and Spotify will look at your previous interactions, and compare those with millions of other users to suggest other items you may wish to purchase, or other artists you may like. This is done to drive follow-on sales or to promote continued interaction with the app.

1.14 Cloud computing and cloud accounting

Cloud computing: The provision of computing as a consumable service instead of a purchased product. It enables data, system information and software to be accessed by computers remotely as a utility through the internet.

Cloud accounting: The provision of accountancy software through the cloud. Users log in to the accountancy software to process financial transactions and produce management reports in the same way as if the software was installed on their own machine.

A cloud can be private or public. A **public cloud** sells services to anyone on the internet. A **private cloud** is a proprietary network or a data centre that supplies hosted services to a limited number of people or organisations.

When a service provider uses public cloud resources to create their private cloud, the result is called a **virtual private cloud**. The goal of cloud computing is to provide easy, scalable access to computing resources and IT services.

A cloud computing service has distinct characteristics that differentiate it from traditional hosting:

- **Sold on demand** – Users pay for cloud services only when they use them, eg by the day, month, or year.
- **Elastic** – Users can have as much or as little of the service as they want at any given time.
- **Fully managed** – The service is fully managed by the service provider. The user just needs an internet connection to access it.
- **On-demand and self-service** – The service is available all the time and the user operates the service themselves.

1.15 Impacts of the cloud on the finance function

Finance functions use cloud computing in a similar way to other parts of the business. Files and software can be stored in cloud servers so that they can be easily shared by all users and accessed by employees whether they are located in the organisation's offices or not.

Cloud computing is changing the structure and working of the finance function by:

- Allowing **flexible working** as staff can work in different locations at different times
- Allowing **collaboration** as files can be shared and updated by multiple staff in real-time
- Keeping software continuously **up-to-date** and improving compliance with data protection regulations
- Improving the **integration** of software as, for example, customer relationship management software can be linked to accounting software
- Improving **data security** as cloud providers better understand how to protect data

Examples of providers of cloud accounting software include QuickBooks, Xero and Sage.

A key **benefit** of cloud accounting is that it supports the various finance components to work as a team. Data, such as underlying transactions, is shared and drives the reports and analysis produced by all the teams. Management can quickly and easily pull data from the system to monitor the financial performance of the organisation themselves without have to wait for accounts and reports to be produced.

The **limitations** around cloud accounting include:

- A reliance on third party providers
- A loss of control over a key system
- Reliance on a strong internet connection to access the system

Activity 1: Novel technologies

Which of the following novel technologies increases the speed at which data and information reach decision makers?

(1) Big data

(2) Blockchain

(3) Data visualisation

(4) Artificial intelligence

	✓
1 and 2 only	
1, 3 and 4 only	
3 and 4 only	
All of them	

1.16 Outsourcing and offshoring

> **Outsourcing:** An organisation subcontracts business activities to external providers.
>
> **Offshoring:** Relocation of part of an organisation's activities to another country.

In order to cut costs, improve efficiencies or focus on core competencies organisations can subcontract certain services to other companies. Common areas of outsourcing include:

- **Cleaning** – Hospitals and schools commonly outsource this so they can focus on healthcare and education.
- **Manufacturing** – Companies sometimes focus on design then outsource manufacturing overseas (offshoring) to take advantage of cheaper labour costs.
- **Debt collection** – Some companies use debt factoring to deal with invoicing and cash collection.
- **IT services** – Companies with low internal technology competencies may use specialist service providers, eg cloud computing services.

1.17 Advantages and disadvantages of outsourcing

The general advantages of outsourcing include:

- **Focus on core competencies** – Outsourced activities are often peripheral to an organisations main purpose.
- **Save costs** – It can be cheaper for one outsourcing company to clean 100 schools than 100 schools to employ a cleaning team each.
- **Keep up-to-date** – Outsourced companies are specialists, eg an IT provider may provide the latest in technology services, and will need to keep up-to-date to remain competitive.

The disadvantages can include:

- **Lack of control** – Even non-core activities can be crucial, and these are being provided by a third-party eg if a hospital is not cleaned properly this failure will be blamed on the hospital even though they don't do the cleaning themselves.
- **Existing staff** – Internal staff will lose their jobs. They may face redundancy, or, be transferred to the outsourcing company.
- **Lack of skills** – If the organisation decided to bring services back 'in house' at a later date it will lack the staff and skills to do this quickly.

Crucial to the success of any outsourcing arrangement will be the **Service Level Agreement (SLA)**. This will be a detailed contract stipulating the level of service to be provided, measured by a range of Key Performance Indicators (KPIs).

1.18 Impacts of outsourcing and offshoring

The wider **impacts of outsourcing** and **offshoring** can include:

- **Changes to the organisational structure** – Internal departments are now replaced with external providers.

- **Impact on cost structures** – Internal departments tend to have large fixed costs bases. Outsource arrangements can be a mix of fixed and variable costs, eg you may only pay for the services you use, subject to any fixed fees for ongoing support.
- **Closer to markets** – Production can be moved closer to where goods are made or sold. For instance a company in the UK that sells in Asia can continue to design in the UK but move production to Asia to benefit from lower costs and closer market access.
- **Better markets** – Activities can be moved to more suitable locations, eg to take advantage of lower tax regimes, better technology etc.

2 Data protection and security

The data protection laws, such as the UK's **Data Protection Act 2018** (TSO, 2018), aim to protect individuals, not companies, from misuse of information being held on computer-based and manual information systems.

They often just apply to **personal data**, ie data which may identify an individual. This includes facts and opinions about the individual.

In order to protect the individual, these data protection principles must be complied with:

(a) **Lawfulness, fairness, and transparency** – There must be valid grounds for holding the data.

(b) **Purpose limitation** – The purpose for recording the data must be recorded and made clear to the data subject from the start.

(c) **Data minimisation** – The data held data must be adequate (sufficient to fulfil the purpose), relevant (linked rationally to the purpose) and not excessive

(d) **Accuracy** – Reasonable steps must be taken to ensure the data is not incorrect or misleading.

(e) **Storage limitation** – Data should not be kept for longer than is necessary for the purpose for which it was processed.

(f) **Integrity and confidentiality** – Data processing must take appropriate security measures as regards risks that might arise. Appropriate technical and organisational measures should be in place to protect the data.

(g) **Accountability** - organisations and individuals should take responsibility for how they collect and use personal data and for compliance with the other principles. There must be appropriate policies and records in place to prove compliance.

2.1 Processing data

Organisations that process personal data are known as **Data controllers. Data processors** are responsible for processing personal data on behalf of a controller. **Data subjects** are identified or identifiable individuals (not companies) to whom personal data relates.

Data controllers and processors are accountable to **The Information Commissioner**, the UK's regulator for data protection. The Information Commissioner has powers to enforce compliance with the law and must be informed within 72 hours of a data breach that affects the rights and freedoms of individuals. In high-risk cases, the individuals affected must be notified as well.

Non-compliance with the Act may result in:

- A **criminal conviction** where a criminal offence has been committed under the Act (for example for the re-identification of data with an individual after it had been anonymised)
- A **fine** of up to £18m or 4% of the organisation's global turnover imposed by the Information Commissioner

Illustration 3: Data security

TV presenter Jeremy Clarkson lost money after publishing his bank details in his newspaper column. The former Top Gear host revealed his account numbers after rubbishing the furore over the loss of 25 million people's personal details on two computer discs. He wanted to prove the story was a fuss about nothing.

Clarkson admitted he was wrong after he discovered a reader had used the details to create a £500 direct debit to the charity, Diabetes UK. Clarkson published details of his bank account in his weekly newspaper column, including details of his account number and sort code. He even told people how to find out his address.

Analysis

Clarkson acknowledged his mistake in his next column, pointing out that the Data Protection Act itself prevented the bank from telling him who had set up the direct debit on his behalf.

Activity 2: Data Protection

Sarah Conner is a data subject of Pest Terminators Ltd. She has some concerns over the way her personal data is being held and processed by her employer.

Required

Which TWO of the following statements are true?

	✓
The company can be fined for non-compliance.	
The company may hold data for whatever period they deem necessary.	
The company may freely transfer Sarah's data to their Brazilian subsidiary.	
Sarah can demand that the company correct any inaccurate data held about her.	

2.2 Cyber risks and cyber security

Cyber-attacks are a major data security risk and come in many forms. These risks can be mitigated through the use of cyber security systems.

2.3 Cyber attacks

Cyber-attacks can include:

Cyber-attack methods	Description
Phishing	The cyber-attacker sends emails to the victim which appear to be from a trusted source, for example a bank. The emails request the victim sends back security information (such as usernames and passwords) and personal details and uses them to steal funds from the victim.
Pharming	The cyber-attacker targets an organisation's website by automatically redirecting visitors from the organisation's website to a bogus website. The intention is to collect data in order to commit fraud and is similar to phishing.
Hacking	The cyber-attacker uses specialist software and other tools to gain unauthorised access to an organisation's computer system and take administrative control. Such control allows them to view and copy system records, as well as amend or delete information that they find. Some hackers may try to stop the system working altogether.

Cyber-attack methods	Description
Distributed denial of service attack (DDoS)	The cyber-attacker attempts to disrupt an organisation's online activities by preventing people from accessing the organisation's website. Bots are instructed to overwhelm the organisation's website with a wave of internet traffic so that the system is unable to handle it and may crash.
Webcam manager	The cyber-attacker uses software to take control of the user's webcam.
File hijacker / ransomware	The cyber-attacker gains access to the user's system to hijack their files and hold them to ransom.
Keylogging	The cyber-attacker plants software onto the user's computer to record what the user types onto their keyboard. The objective is to learn passwords and user details to gain access to confidential information.
Screenshot manager	The cyber-attacker plants software onto the user's computer allowing them to take screenshots. This can deliver access to sensitive information stored on their system.
Ad clicker	The cyber-attacker directs the victim's computer to a bogus website by encouraging them to click on a specific link contained in online advertising.

2.4 Cyber security

The most common types of cyber security include:

- **Access controls** – passwords or locked doors to prevent access to systems
- **Boundary firewalls** – software to regulate/monitor access to internal systems by outside sources
- **Malware protection** – software to prevent hacking tools being uploaded to systems
- **Patch management** – uploads to fix security issues with existing software

Chapter summary

The finance function gather data, transform it into information, and analyse it for insights. This is done to supply information for decision making at the strategic, managerial, and operational levels of management.

Good quality information has characteristics that can be summarised with the mnemonic ACCURATE.

New technologies that can assist the finance function include:

- Process automation
- Blockchain; a form of distributed ledger technology
- Artificial intelligence
- Electronic signatures and filing
- Big data and data analytics
- Cloud computing and cloud accounting

Mobile technologies and the internet have also facilitated an extension of outsourcing and offshoring whereby organisations can subcontract non-core activities to experts, or move these processes overseas. These can have an impact on:

- Organisational structures
- Cost structures
- Markets and locations

Data Protection in the UK is regulated by the Information Commissioner. The main data protection principles are:

- Lawfulness, fairness, and transparency
- Purpose limitation
- Data minimisation
- Accuracy
- Storage limitation
- Integrity and confidentiality
- Accountability

Data processors and controllers are accountable for data protection and face severe fines for non-compliance.

Cyber-attacks are a major threat to data security. Threats include hacking, phishing, pharming, DDoS, webcam and screenshot managers, keylogging, ransomware, and ad clickers.

Common cyber security measures include:

- Access controls
- Boundary firewalls
- Malware protection
- Patch management

Activity answers

Activity 1: Novel technologies

The correct answer is:

	✓
1 and 2 only	
1, 3 and 4 only	✓
3 and 4 only	
All of them	

Big data increases speed because data can be streamed in real time.

Data visualisations increase speed because they automatically generate information from data (often in real time) and therefore avoid the need for a human to create the information and presentation first.

Artificial intelligence can speed up data flows as machines can learn patterns and deliver relevant information faster and faster as they learn.

Blockchain does not increase speed of data, instead it increases the trust decision makers have in it.

Activity 2: Data Protection

The correct answers are:

	✓
The company can be fined for non-compliance.	✓
The company may hold data for whatever period they deem necessary.	
The company may freely transfer Sarah's data to their Brazilian subsidiary.	
Sarah can demand that the company correct any inaccurate data held about her.	✓

Companies can be fined for non-compliance, and any inaccurate data held must be corrected.

Data cannot be held indefinitely – only for as long as is necessary. Transfer to Brazil would be strictly controlled.

 **BPP**

Test your learning

1 **Complete the sentence**

At the [   ] level of management information is largely unstructured and externally focused.

2 **Which THREE of the following are characteristics of good quality information?**

	✓
Available	
Cost effective	
Understandable	
Technical	
Accessible	

3 **Blockchain is an example of?**

	✓
Cryptocurrency	
Artificial intelligence	
Distributed ledger technology	
Big data	

4 **What are the five Vs of Big Data?**

5 **Describe THREE of the data protection principles.**

Communicating data

Learning outcomes

5.2   **Visualising information**
Learners need to understand:

5.2.1   The importance of being able to visualise information in different formats:
- Images
- Charts
- Diagrams
- Tables
- Matrices
- Graphs

5.2.2   Patterns or significant anomalies within data

5.2.3   The importance of choosing the most appropriate forms of visualised data for communication purposes

5.2.4   That accounting software packages use dashboards to communicate to non-technical stakeholders

Learners need to be able to:

5.2.5   Interpret visual information to indicate relationships and trends

5.3   **Communicating information**
Learners need to understand:

5.3.1   The principles used to determine the appropriate method of communication to use both internally and externally by the business

5.3.2   The characteristics of professional communication:
- Meeting different stakeholder requirements
- Use of appropriate communication medium for desired outcome
- Importance of communicating valid information
- Importance of confidentiality

Assessment context

Questions in the assessment are likely to focus on either identifying which communication tools are appropriate when, or, asking you to interpret visualised data.

Qualification context

At Level 2 in *The Business Environment* you learned about 'producing work in appropriate formats and communicating effectively'.

At Level 4 in *Drafting and Interpreting Financial Statements* you will be required to 'communicate the key findings of their analysis to meet user requirements' in respect of ratio analysis.

Business context

Organisations communicate with a wide range of internal and external stakeholders. It is therefore vital that a range of communication tools are used to ensure each recipient get the information they require in the format that suits their needs.

Chapter overview

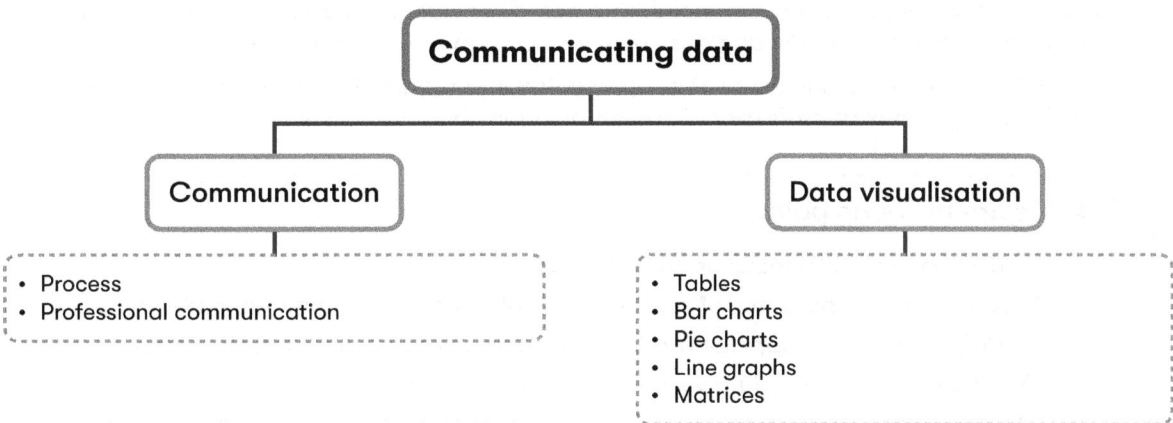

Introduction

You have seen in earlier chapters that the finance function plays a crucial role in the information processes of an organisation. Financial, and non-financial information is crucial in monitoring the performance of the business, and of course for decision making purposes.

Information however is only useful if it is presented in a format that the user can understand, so, in this chapter you look at professional communications and data visualisations.

Assessment focus point

Exam questions will likely focus on the aspects:

(a) Explaining the importance of professional skills in business communications

(b) Identifying the most appropriate form of communication in a given scenario

(c) Describing the various data visualisation tools available

(d) Identifying the most appropriate data visualisation tools to use in a given scenario

(e) Interpreting a data set you have been supplied with, identifying trends and patterns within

---

1 Communicating information

1.1 Communication

Communication is, at its most basic, the **transmission or exchange of information**: putting across a message. However, there are many different purposes for doing this:

- To inform: to give people data they require
- To persuade: to get others to agree to, or do, something
- To request: to ask for something
- To confirm: to check that data is correct and that different parties have the same understanding of it
- To build effective working relationships

All of these activities underpin **efficient working** and **constructive working relationships**.

We tend to think of business communication as being undertaken using formal methods, such as emails and reports. However there are also a lot of informal communications eg social conversations. These exchanges are sometimes referred to as 'the grapevine', and such informal chats can be a useful tool for building rapport between employees, though, can also be a source of gossip and conflict.

1.2 The communication process

Effective communication is a two-way process, often shown as a 'cycle'. Signals or messages are sent by the communicator and received by the target recipient, who sends back some form of confirmation that the message has been received and understood. Communication can travel in different directions eg vertically between a manager and their subordinate, horizontally between colleagues, or diagonally between a subordinate and a manager in a different department.

Some means of communication are more appropriate and effective than others in **different business contexts**. If you get the choice of whether to carry out a communication task using a letter, memo, email, report or informal note – or, in real working life, a telephone call or face to face discussion – you will need to consider factors such as whether speed is important; whether there is the need for written confirmation; which format will best support you in getting your message across to the recipient; and which is the most efficient method in terms of time and cost. This is considered in more detail later in this chapter.

1.3 Communicating appropriately

This unit requires you to demonstrate that you can 'determine the most appropriate method of communication to use both internally and externally'. So what makes communication appropriate'?

Attribute	Explanation
Using appropriate formats	Selecting the right format (letter, email, memorandum etc) for the job
Observing format conventions and house style	Using formats correctly: observing conventions of structure, format and style, within organisational guidelines and 'house style'
Professionally presented	Ensuring that documents are neat, legible, concise, helpfully structured and smartly presented: showing competence and awareness of business needs
Technically correct	Ensuring that content is accurate, appropriately detailed (for different levels of requirement) and checked for factual/data and typographical errors
Clearly understandable	Tailored to the writer's purpose in communicating (so that a clear message is sent) and to the information needs, language and capabilities of its audience (so that the message can be received)
Projecting the appropriate corporate image	Reflecting a general image of professionalism and competence – including appropriate formality – and the specific desired image or 'character' of the organisation
Achieving its purpose	Obtain feedback to check that the communication has been effective. Has it 'done its job'? Has it got the response it aimed for? If not: adjust and try again!

1.4 Professional communication

In addition to the general principles of communication best practice, **professional communication** requires:

- **Meeting different stakeholder requirements** – For instance, when looking to secure a bank loan a company will often supply their management accounts as well as their published financial statements.
- **Appropriate communications for the desired outcome** – For example, applying for a bank loan will result in the agreement of a formal legal contract. This will need to be supported by other written documents.
- **Communicating valid information** – The bank loan application will require the company to prove it is solvent and can meet the repayment schedule over the term of the loan. This information will be used to secure finance so must be prepared honestly and accurately.
- **Importance of confidentiality** – A loan application will involve the exchange of confidential information. This will require both parties to agree a suitably secure submission method eg excel sheets will need to be password protected, and to take steps to protect any data received in line with data protection laws.

Activity 1: Communication mediums

Suggest the most effective medium for communication in the following situations using the drop down list.

Situation	Medium
New stationery is urgently required from the office goods supplier.	▼
The Managing Director wants to give a message to all staff.	▼
A member of staff has been absent five times in the past month, and her manager intends to take action.	▼
You need information quickly from another department.	▼
You have to explain a complicated procedure to a group of people.	▼

Picklist

- Face-to-face communication
- Face-to-face conversation
- Meeting
- Notice board/intranet
- Telephone

2 Data visualisation

KEY TERM

> **Data visualisation:** The process of presenting report formats that represent data and information in a pictorial or graphical format that helps the recipient to understand the significance of the content more easily than if presented in a traditional report format.

The main impact of data visualisation on organisations is the change that they bring to **how information is presented**. Because data presented in dashboards and mapping charts can be drilled into, they are geared to being presented on tablets and smart devices rather than on paper. This makes reporting quicker and cheaper, and should support the quicker decision-making capabilities required in the modern business environment.

It is important for organisations to provide the necessary technology and training so that staff get the most out of the visualisations and can use them for improved decision making.

2.1 Benefits of data visualisation

Some key **benefits of data visualisation** for the finance function include:
- Accessibility in terms of visual appeal and the ability to be easily understood
- Real-time processing means the picture is always kept up-to-date
- Performance optimisation as clear information allows improved decision making and efficient use of resources in response
- Allows richer insights and understanding of the relationships that drive performance, eg **patterns or anomalies are easily spotted**

2.2 Principles of effective 'graphic' communication

In addition to the **numerical competences** required to organise your data, there are some **key principles** of effective 'graphic' communication.

- Give each diagram or chart a concise and meaningful title.
- Cite the source of the data, where relevant.
- Clearly label all elements of the diagram, either on the diagram itself or in a separate 'key' to the colours or symbols used.
- Keep textual elements (labels, explanatory notes) brief.
- Keep the presentation as simple as possible: cut down on unnecessary lines and elements, to avoid overcrowding, clutter and confusion.

As with any form of communication there is still a risk of **'data overload'** when presenting visualisations. With this in mind when preparing visualisations you should:

- Assess the range of visuals that your **accounting software** can create.
- Identify your target audience. If they are not accountants, then you should select graphics that can best communicate financial terms most clearly in the eyes of **non-financial** workers.
- Choose the **most suitable tools** bearing in mind the messages you are trying to convey. In the next section a range of common visuals are demonstrated.

2.3 Tables

Tables are a good way of organising information. The use of columns and rows allows the data to be classified under appropriate headings, clearly organised and labelled, totalled up in various ways (across rows or down columns) and so on.

You might use a table format to organise data about the unit sales of a company's three main products.

Month 20X5	Product A	Product B	Product C	Total
Jan	600	210	20	830
Feb	625	205	20	850
Mar	640	200	30	870
Apr	660	180	35	875
May	680	210	40	930
Jun	670	230	45	945
Jul	650	180	45	875
Aug	680	170	45	895
Sep	640	150	65	855
Oct	620	120	70	810
Nov	550	120	70	740
Dec	500	115	65	680

2.4 Bar charts

Bar charts are useful for showing or comparing magnitudes or sizes of items: for example, unit sales of each product each month over the financial year. Bar charts are very flexible.

- The diagram needs to be labelled to indicate what it shows.
- The positions of the bars are labelled to show what they represent (eg months or departments).

 **BPP**

- The height of the bars, drawn against a specified scale, indicate the magnitudes of the different items (monetary value or number).
- The bars can be subdivided to show components of the total magnitudes (eg number of different units sold each month).

2.5 Pie charts

Pie charts are useful for showing the relative sizes of component elements of a total value or amount, represented by the 360 degrees of the circle or 'pie'. An example might be showing the breakdown of the time you spend on different tasks during a day, or the breakdown of monthly sales revenue by product or customer. Below are the steps involved in providing a pie chart in relation to this.

Step 1 Calculate each item as a fraction and/or percentage of the whole. (If handling emails takes you five hours out of your 40-hour week, say, that's 5/40 or 1/8 or 12.5%.)

Step 2 Translate each fraction/percentage into fractions of a circle. (The 'slice' occupied by handling emails would be 1/8 of the pie.) If you want to draw very accurately, using geometric instruments, you would calculate the exact number of degrees of the circle occupied by each slice, as a fraction or percentage of 360° (1/8 × 360°= 45°).

Step 3 Draw a circle, and divide it up using the fractions (or, to be more accurate, degrees) calculated for each slice.

Step 4 Label each slice with what it represents, and its percentage of the total. Check that it adds up to 100%.

Using the table of data above, a pie-chart clearly shows the contribution each product is making to total unit sales in the year.

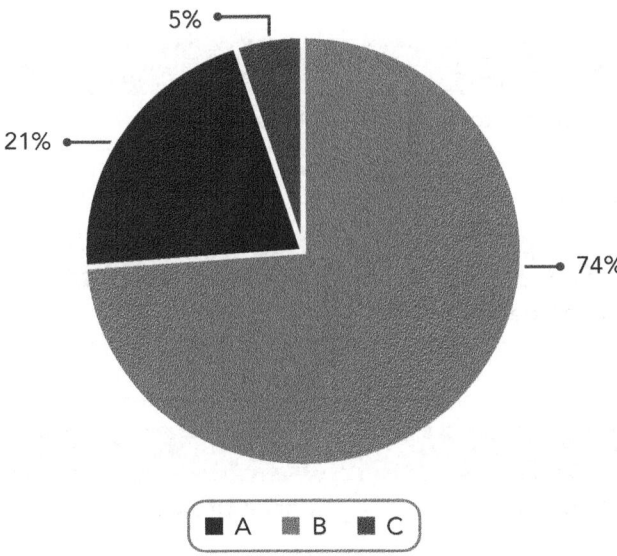

Unit sales contribution by product 20X55

5%
21%
74%

■ A ■ B ■ C

2.6 Line graphs

Line graphs are useful for showing the relationship between two variables (represented by the horizontal and vertical axes of the graph), by plotting points and joining them up with straight or curved lines. These are particularly useful for demonstrating trends, such as the variation in unit sales each month. This can make it easy to see trends over time.

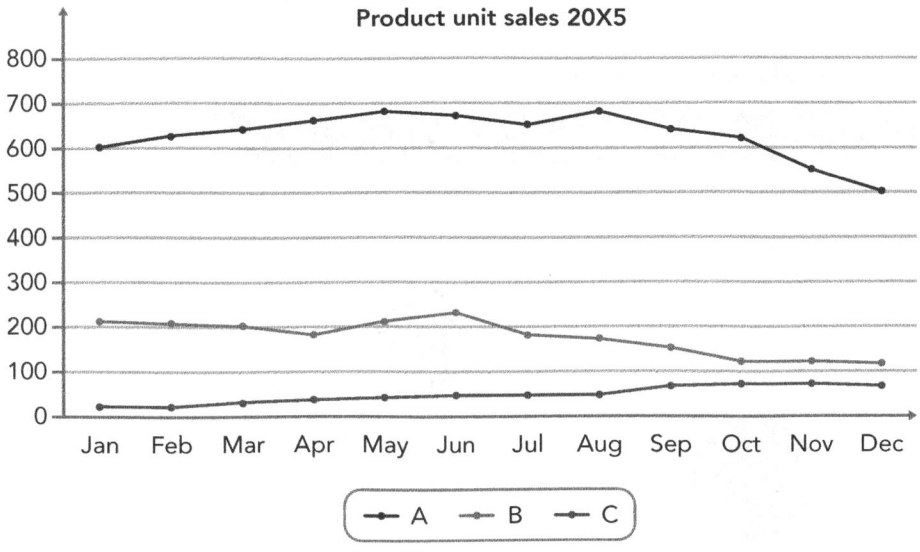

Product unit sales 20X5

—•— A   —•— B   —•— C

This graph shows the variation in sales of each product over the year, highlighting the decline in sales of A and B in the last quarter of the year.

2.7 Matrices

Matrix diagrams show the relationship between items. These allow you to quickly assess the value of certain items relative to each other.

As an example the Boston Consulting Group Matrix allows a company to assess the strength of its product portfolio. It does this by assessing:

(a) The sales of each product relative to its strongest competitor; and

(b) The growth rate of each market.

The result is a diagram that illustrates the categorisation of each item, and whether the company has a balanced portfolio.

By adding some more detail to our original data table you can see how the matrix is developed.

Additional data

Product A		
Sales in 20X5	Strongest competitor	Market growth
7,515	6,055	8%

Product B		
Sales in 20X5	Strongest competitor	Market growth
2,090	4,090	16%

Product C		
Sales in 20X5	Strongest competitor	Market growth
550	440	22%

From this data it is possible to work out the relative market share of each product:

	Product A	Product B	Product C
Relative market share	7,515/6,055 = 1.24	2,090/4,090 = 0.51	550/440 = 1.25
Market growth	8%	16%	22%

This can then be represented in a matrix as follows.

BPP

Chapter summary

The finance function is a key information provider within the organisation. This information needs to be presented in a manner that is appropriate to its recipient.

Communication is a two-way process. Information can pass horizontally, vertically or diagonally.

Appropriateness must take account of:

- Format
- Professionalism
- Technical correctness
- Understandability
- Achieving its purpose

Professional communication means:

- Meeting the needs of all stakeholders
- Appropriate to the desired outcomes
- Communicating valid information
- Respecting confidentiality

Data Visualisation means presenting information is a graphical form. This can comprise a dashboard featuring:

- Images
- Charts
- Diagrams
- Tables
- Matrices
- Graphs

 BPP

Activity answers

Activity 1: Communication mediums

Situation	Medium
New stationery is urgently required from the office goods supplier.	Telephone – fast
The Managing Director wants to give a message to all staff.	Notice board/intranet – needs to be accessible by all staff. Also want a permanent record.
A member of staff has been absent five times in the past month, and her manager intends to take action.	Face-to-face conversation Disciplinary actions always requires a face-to-face meeting, with any warnings backed up in writing afterwards.
You need information quickly from another department.	Telephone – this is fast and direct. Unlike email it ensures instant receipt of the message.
You have to explain a complicated procedure to a group of people.	Meeting – groups lend themselves to meetings. Although email might be used a meeting allows questions and feedback to be shared, which is useful here as the procedure is 'complicated'.

Test your learning

1 Complete the following sentence using the picklist below.

[▼] is the response of a person with whom you are communicating, which indicates whether your message has (or has not) been received and understood as you intended.

Picklist

- Budget control
- Exception reporting
- Feedback
- Feedforward

2 For each of the following situations, which would be the most appropriate method of communication? Choose from the picklist below.

Situation	Method
Detailing a telephone message left by a supplier for a colleague	▼
Informing an employee that his work has not been up to standard recently	▼
Requesting a customer's sales ledger account balance from the credit controller	▼
Requesting production details for the last month from the factory manager where the factory is situated five miles away	▼
Sending monthly variances to the sales manager	▼

Picklist

- Email
- Face-to-face discussion
- Informal note

3 You have been looking at a presentation which the assistant management accountant is preparing. The pie chart below looks fine, but it would be helpful if there were some numbers. These appear to have been missed off.

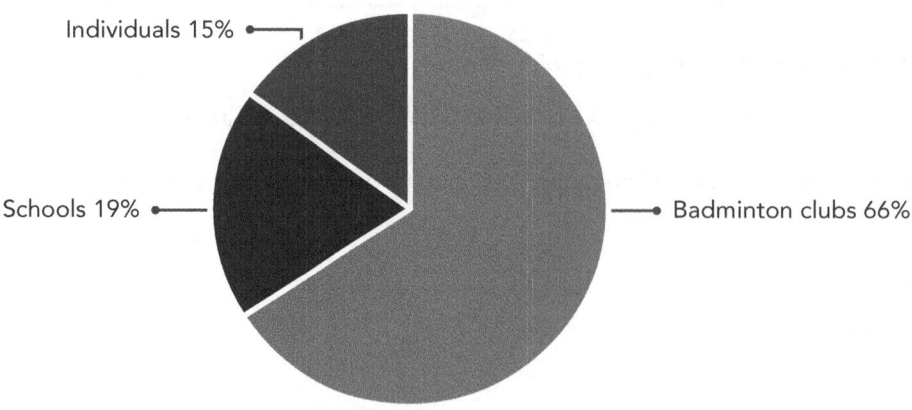

Racquet sales for 20X9

Individuals 15%

Schools 19%

Badminton clubs 66%

Required

Using the percentages from the pie chart, fill in the sales figures below.

	Sales £
Badminton clubs	
Schools	
Individuals	
Total	650,912

4 If a manager in the purchasing department requests the help of the Human Resources Director in preparing for a difficult appraisal, what direction is the communication flow?

	✓
Vertical	
Horizontal	
Diagonal	

5 Which THREE of the following will influence the medium of communication that should be used in any given situation?

	✓
Permanency	
Necessity	
Complexity	
Severity	
Urgency	

 BPP

Test your learning answers

Chapter 1

1 Three different aims that an organisation might have when it is created include:
- The pursuit of profit
- Charitable aims
- Non-profit

2 Services have the following qualities:
- Intangibility – The service does not provide a physical product.
- Inseparability – The service is usually provided at the same time as it is consumed.
- Variability – The service is tailored to the needs of each individual customer.
- Perishability – The service cannot be stored and used later.

3 The correct answer is:

	✓
All partners will receive profits in line with their capital contribution.	✓
All partners will have access to the firm's books.	
All partners will take part in the management of the firm.	
All partners will be indemnified for any liabilities.	

In the absence of a partnership agreement document all partners will receive an equal share of partnership profits.

4 The correct answers are:

	✓
Duty to account for monies received.	✓
Duty to promote the long-term success of the company.	
Duty to exercise reasonable, skill, care and diligence.	
Duty to disclose.	✓

Fiduciary duties are:
- A duty to account for any monies/goods/services received
- Avoid a conflict of interest
- Duty to disclose
- Not to make a secret profit

The other duties are statutory in nature.

5 The correct answer is:

	✓
Shareholders are personally liable for the debts of the company.	
Directors are personally liable for the debts of the company.	
Shareholders and directors are both personally liable for the debts of the company.	
Neither shareholders nor directors are personally liable for the debts of the company.	✓

One of the benefits of a company is that it alone is liable for its debts – This arises from the veil of incorporation.

Chapter 2

1 The correct answer is:

	✓
Divisional	
Functional	
Matrix	✓

A matrix organisation crosses a functional structure with a product/customer/project structure. This would be appropriate in an organisation where work is mainly project based.

2 A ⟨narrow⟩ span of control will result in long scalar chain.

3 The correct answer is:

	✓
Faster decisions	
Holistic view of the organisation	
More standardisation	
Increased motivation of junior managers	✓

The other options are advantages of centralised structures.

4 The correct answer is:

	✓
Strategic risks	
Operational risks	✓
Business risks	
Non-business risks	

All of other options are types of strategic risks, cyber-risks are categorised as operational risks.

5   Stakeholders can be classified as:

*   Primary – those directly affected by a decision, eg owners, managers, and staff of a company.

*   Secondary – those indirectly affected by a decision, who may still be able to exert some influence over the company.

Chapter 3

1

Factor	Element of PESTLE
Unemployment levels	**Social –** this is a particular challenge for governments; high unemployment is a drag on economic productivity
Changes in disposable income	**Economic –** the net effect of interest rates, inflation, taxation polices will impact the available money consumers have to spend on necessities and luxuries
Sustainability	**Environmental –** consumers are increasingly aware of the impact that their consumption is having on the planet
Trade regulations	**Legal –** laws that are directed at specific industries can be highly disruptive

2   The law of ⏢demand⏢ : As the price of a good falls, all other things being equal, the quantity

demanded of that good ⏢increases⏢ .

3   The correct answer is:

	✓
Normal goods	
Superior goods	
Substitutes	
Inferior goods	✓

An inferior good is one where buyers buy less as their income increases.

4   The law of supply: 'As the price of a good rises, all other things being equal, the quantity supplied of that good increases'.

5   The correct answers can include:

Overcoming short-term views – companies focus on short-term profit, sustainability can be a long-term investment. Overcoming negative stakeholder reactions – some may be negative.

Using resources sustainably – can a process that uses finite resources be altered to be sustainable?

Managing the holistic impacts – the consequences of some sustainability actions can be far-reaching eg impact through the supply chain.

Chapter 4

1 The AAT's Code of Ethics provides ‎‏ a conceptual framework ‎‏ which members must apply to enable them to identify and evaluate threats to compliance with the fundamental principles and to respond appropriately to them.

2 The correct answers are:

	✓
Potential for consistent actions	
Guidelines can become de-facto rules	✓
Potential for subjective interpretations	✓
Removes loopholes which can be exploited	

The disadvantages of the principles-based approach include:

- Can lead to subjective interpretations of guidelines
- Potential for inconsistent actions
- Guidelines can become de-facto rules

3 The correct answer is:

	✓
Objectivity	✓
Professional behaviour	
Integrity	
Confidentiality	

Objectivity refers to the ability to make judgements and decisions free from bias, and within this the guidelines also make it clear that you are expected to avoid situations that cause a conflict of interest to arise.

4 Professional scepticism is the attitude that includes a questioning mind, being alert to conditions which may indicate possible misstatement due to error or fraud, and a critical assessment of evidence.

5 The correct answer is:

	✓
Integrity	✓
Confidentiality	
Professional competence	
Professional behaviour	

Familiarity – the threat that due to a long or close relationship with a client or employer, a professional accountant will be too sympathetic to their interests. This represents a threat to integrity, eg the accountant covers up mistakes made by a friend.

Chapter 5

1 The correct answers are:

	✓
Businesses	✓
The AAT	✓
The accounting profession	✓
The accountant	✓

Unethical behaviour can harm corporate reputations, the AAT, the wider accountancy profession and the reputation and career prospects of the accountant at fault.

2 The correct answers are:

	✓
Transparent investigation	✓
Consider all parties affected	✓
Punishing wrong doers	
Cover-up to protect reputations	
Fairness in the process	✓

When dealing with such matters, the organisation should try and ensure:

- Transparency – Do you feel comfortable about the decision made, are your actions justifiable?
- Effect – Have all affected parties been considered, all stakeholders considered?
- Fairness – Would a rational bystander consider the outcomes to be fair?

3 If you are accused of acting unethically the AAT may call a Disciplinary Tribunal hearing. You will be given ⏐ 42 ⏐ days' notice of such a meeting.

Unethical action on your behalf can be reported to the AAT which could result in a Disciplinary Tribunal hearing. In these instances you will be given 42 days' notice of a hearing.

4 The correct answer is:

	✓
Higher of 2.5 times gross fee income or £50,000	
Higher of 2.5 times gross fee income or £100,000	✓
£50,000	
£100,00	

The level of cover required is:

- **Sole traders** – higher of: 2.5 times the firm's gross fee income, or £50,000
- **Partnerships** - higher of: 2.5 times the firm's gross fee income, or £100,000
- **Limited companies** - higher of: 2.5 times the firm's gross fee income, or £100,000

5 The penalties for accountants found guilty of money laundering are:

- **Laundering** – a maximum 14-year prison sentence is possible, and/or a fine. Additionally, the police may seize the illegitimate assets
- **Failure to report** – punishable by a maximum five-year sentence and/or a fine
- **Tipping off** – punishable by a maximum two-year sentence and/or a fine

Chapter 6

1 At the ⌈strategic⌉ level of management information is largely unstructured and externally focused.

2 The correct answers are:

	✓
Available	
Cost effective	✓
Understandable	✓
Technical	
Accessible	✓

Good quality information should be: **A**ccurate; **C**ost-effective, **C**omplete, **U**nderstandable, **R**elevant, **A**ccessible, **T**imely, **E**asy-to-use.

3 The correct answer is:

	✓
Cryptocurrency	
Artificial intelligence	
Distributed ledger technology	✓
Big data	

 BPP

Blockchain is a form of a distributed ledger system. Distributed ledgers are a technology that allows organisations and individuals who are unconnected to share an agreed record of events, such as ownership of an asset.

4 **Volume** – the quantity of data that is available

   Velocity – the speed at which big data can be accessed by an organisation

   Variety – the different forms that big data can take

   Veracity – the trustworthiness or accuracy of big data

   Value – the ability of big data to add value to an organisation

5 You could choose any THREE of the following.

   (1) **Lawfulness, fairness, and transparency** – There must be valid grounds for holding the data.

   (2) **Purpose limitation** – The purpose for recording the data must be recorded and made clear to the data subject from the start.

   (3) **Data minimisation** – The data held data must be adequate (sufficient to fulfil the purpose), relevant (linked rationally to the purpose) and not excessive

   (4) **Accuracy** – Reasonable steps must be taken to ensure the data is not incorrect or misleading.

   (5) **Storage limitation** – Data should not be kept for longer than is necessary for the purpose for which it was processed.

   (6) **Integrity and confidentiality** – Data processing must take appropriate security measures as regards risks that might arise. Appropriate technical and organisational measures should be in place to protect the data.

   (7) **Accountability** – organisations and individuals should take responsibility for how they collect and use personal data and for compliance with the other principles. There must be appropriate policies and records in place to prove compliance

Chapter 7

1 Feedback   is the response of a person with whom you are communicating, which indicates

   whether your message has (or has not) been received and understood as you intended.

   Feedback is important in enabling you to adjust your message, if necessary, in order to ensure that the message has been received, and that there are no misunderstandings.

2

Situation	Method
Detailing a telephone message left by a supplier for a colleague	Informal note
Informing an employee that his work has not been up to standard recently	Face-to-face discussion
Requesting a customer's sales ledger account balance from the credit controller	Email
Requesting production details for the last month from the factory manager where the factory is situated five miles away	Email
Sending monthly variances to the sales manager	Email

*A face-to-face discussion is necessary because of the sensitivity of the issue, and the need for interactive question and answer.

3

	Sales £
Badminton clubs	429,602
Schools	123,673
Individuals	97,637
Total	650,912

4 The correct answer is:

	✓
Vertical	
Horizontal	
Diagonal	✓

The manager is in a different function and also below the director.

5 The correct answers are:

	✓
Permanency	✓
Necessity	
Complexity	✓
Severity	
Urgency	✓

Permanency: the need for a written record for legal evidence, confirmation of a transaction for future reference.

Complexity: for example the need for a graphic illustration to explain concepts.

Urgency: the speed of transition.

In addition, the choice of medium is also affected by the sensitivity/confidentiality of the message, the ease of dissemination and the cost effectiveness of the communication method.

Glossary

Chapter 1: Types of businesses

Business: A business is defined as an organisation or enterprising entity engaged in commercial, industrial, or professional activities. Businesses can be for-profit entities or they can be non-profit organisations that operate to fulfil a charitable mission or further a social cause.

Goodwill: An intangible asset that is associated with the purchase of one business by another.

Incorporation: The legal process used to form a corporate entity or company. A corporation is the resulting legal entity that separates the firm's assets and income from its owners and investors.

Organisation: A social arrangement which pursues collective goals, controls its own performance and which has a boundary separating it from its environment. Boundaries can be physical or social.

Chapter 2: Organisational structure and governance

Corporate governance: The system by which companies are directed and controlled. It considers how directors can be held accountable to shareholders for their actions.

Risk: The condition in which there exists a quantifiable dispersion in the possible outcomes from any activity', ie the possibility that actual results will turn out differently from those expected.

Scalar chain: The number of links between the board and the most junior employees.

Span of control: The number of subordinates that a manager can manage.

Stakeholder: A person or group of persons who have a stake in the organisation.

Uncertainty: The inability to predict the outcome from an activity due to a lack of information about the input/output relationship or about the environment within which the activity takes place.

Chapter 3: The external environment

Equilibrium price: The price at which quantity demanded and quantity supplied will be equal, and which will be restored by market forces following any changes in the conditions of either supply or demand.

Macro-environment: The condition that exists in the economy as a whole, rather than in a particular sector or region. In general, the macro economic environment includes trends in the gross domestic product (GDP), inflation, employment, spending, and monetary and fiscal policy.

The law of demand: As the price of a good falls, all other things being equal, the quantity demanded of that good increases.

The law of supply: As the price of a good rises, all other things being equal, the quantity supplied of that good increases.

Chapter 4: Professional ethics for accountants

Confidentiality: There is a duty to safeguard any information in your possession unless there is a legal or professional duty to disclose. This is an area that strays from ethics into law and in order to bring clarity to this area, AAT has provided a list of examples where confidential information can be disclosed:

(a) When permitted by law

(b) When permitted by the client or employer

(c) When required by law

(d) When permitted by a professional duty or right

Integrity: An individual should act in a manner that is **honest** and **straightforward** in all professional and business relationships. This extends beyond the work that an accountant produces and extends to the manner in which they **conduct** themselves.

Objectivity: The ability to make judgements and decisions **free from bias**. Within this the guidelines also make it clear that you are expected to avoid situations that cause a **conflict of interest** to arise.

Professional behaviour: Not doing anything that will discredit AAT or the wider accounting profession. This is defined as 'actions which a reasonable and informed third party, having knowledge of all relevant information, would conclude negatively affects the good reputation of the profession'.

Professional competence and due care: An accountant should only take on tasks which they are **technically competent** to perform. There is also a duty to **take reasonable care** and remain **technically up-to-date**.

Professional scepticism: An attitude that includes a questioning mind, being alert to conditions which may indicate possible misstatement due to error or fraud, and a critical assessment of evidence.

Chapter 5: Ethical conflicts

Money laundering: The process by which the proceeds of crime, which have illegitimate origins, are converted into assets that appear to be legitimate.

Chapter 6: Technology and data

Artificial intelligence: The ability of a computer system to assist to perform cognitive tasks such as making business decisions, finding patterns in data, or helping solve problems.

Big data: The vast volumes of data which are captured from various sources, such as web browsing and the internet of things that can be analysed to reveal patterns or trends, especially relating to human behaviour or interactions.

Blockchain: A form of a distributed ledger system.

Cloud accounting: The provision of accountancy software through the cloud. Users log in to the accountancy software to process financial transactions and produce management reports in the same way as if the software was installed on their own machine.

Cloud computing: The provision of computing as a consumable service instead of a purchased product. It enables data, system information and software to be accessed by computers remotely as a utility through the internet.

Data analytics: The collection, management and analysis of large data sets with the objective of discovering useful information that an organisation can use for decision making.

Distributed ledger technology: A technology that allows organisations and individuals who are unconnected to share an agreed record of events, such as ownership of an asset.

Offshoring: Relocation of part of an organisation's activities to another country.

Outsourcing: An organisation subcontracts business activities to external providers.

Process automation: The ability of systems to perform routine activities (such as the processing of data and assembling electronic components) without the input of a human.

Chapter 7: Communicating data

Data visualisation: The process of presenting report formats that represent data and information in a pictorial or graphical format that helps the recipient to understand the significance of the content more easily than if presented in a traditional report format.

Bibliography

Association of Accounting Technicians (2017) AAT Code of Professional Ethics. [Online.] Available from: https://www.aat.org.uk/prod/s3fs-public/assets/AAT-Code-Professional-Ethics.pdf [Accessed 19 October 2021].

Companies Act 2006. (2006). London, TSO.

Data Protection Act 2018. (2018). London, TSO.

Financial Reporting Council (July 2018) The UK Corporate Governance Code. [Online]. Available from: https://www.frc.org.uk/getattachment/88bd8c45-50ea-4841-95b0-d2f4f48069a2/2018-UK-Corporate-Governance-Code-FINAL.pdf [Accessed 19 October 2021].

Limited Liability Partnership Act 2000. (2000). London, TSO.

Limited Partnership Act 1907. (1907). London. HMSO.

Partnership Act 1890. (1890). London, HMSO.

Proceeds of Crime Act 2002. (2002). London, TSO.

Index

 BPP

Tell us what you think

Got comments or feedback on this book? Let us know.
Use your QR code reader:

Or, visit:
https://bppgroup.fra1.qualtrics.com/jfe/form/SV_9YwIGE0eqAS5G1E

Need to get in touch with customer service?

www.bpp.com/request-support

Spotted an error?

www.bpp.com/learningmedia/Errata